Through The Wilderness

Finding God's Presence When All Seems Lost

Carol A. Brown

LIGHTSMITH PUBLISHERS

Thorne Bay, Alaska

Copyright © 2016 by Carol A. Brown.

All rights reserved. No part of this publication may be reproduced, distributed or transmitted in any form or by any means, including photocopying, recording, or other electronic or mechanical methods, without the prior written permission of the publisher, except in the case of brief quotations embodied in critical reviews and certain other noncommercial uses permitted by copyright law. For permission requests, write to the publisher, addressed "Attention: Permissions Coordinator," at the address below.

Lightsmith Publishers
P.O. Box 19293
Thorne Bay, AK 99919
www.LightsmithPublishers.com

Ordering Information:
Quantity sales. Special discounts are available on quantity purchases by corporations, associations, and others. For details, contact the "Special Sales Department" at the address above.

Through The Wilderness/ Carol A. Brown. -- 1st ed.
ISBN-10:1-944798-03-X
ISBN-13:978-1-944798-03-1

To all the weary pilgrims—there is a way through!

CONTENTS

Part One THE PATH

1 Different Not Ruined
2 On The Shelf
3 The Trouble With Centering
4 On Brokenness

Part Two THE VISIONS

1 Regaining My Balance
2 The Importance Of Intercession
3 Stained Glass Window
4 Stay The Course
5 No Fears

Part Three HIS VOICE

1 The Joy Of The Lord
2 No Regrets
3 My Mystery Shelf
4 My Long Sleep
5 Camel Hair Shirt

Dear Reader...

In A Quiet Place

Part One
THE PATH

Different, Not Ruined

I slid off the exam table with the doctor's diagnosis ringing in my ears. "We will schedule an MRI, but it will only confirm my diagnosis. I am ninety-nine point nine percent sure that you have MS." I can't remember what I said at that moment, but by the end of the day my resolve was, "I am in no hurry to receive my healing. I want to learn everything the Lord can teach me through this disease. I do not want to have to do another lap around The Sinai, thank you very much." No, I did not want to end up like the children of Israel and spend forty years in my wilderness.

It was December of 1995, when I was diagnosed with multiple sclerosis. Back then, I tended to define myself to others by what I did. I believed, as many do, that my worth depended on my job, on how much money I made, or on how much I could produce each day. Like any propaganda, if you say it enough, you come to believe it. My culture lied to me.

My job did not define me; my value did not depend on what I produced or contributed. This chronic disease brought me an identity crisis that was devastating. When my body no longer looked or functioned as it did, and I was unable to be what I was before—who then was I? What purpose did I have? What was my value to myself and others?

MS tends to shrink life, lopping off huge chunks. It chips away and chips away. Insidious! Now life looked nothing like what I had worked so hard to attain. The attack affected my vision. My ability to read was limited —for a teacher that was the end of a career. The end of being productive. Even if the eye problems were to heal, my energies were so fickle I could not count on them being there on demand. My ability to walk was impaired. Forget about graceful, I was thankful to the Lord that I could walk at all! Should I insist that my body function after it told me to stop, it rewarded me with excruciating exhaustion. It tore at my insides and demanded that I become horizontal—now! Little things required huge outpourings of energy and quickly become too much.

After my diagnosis, I quickly lost interest in trying to do much of anything. Sitting and watching others function normally wreaked havoc on how I saw myself. My name had been synonymous with responsibility and conscientiousness, and suddenly I was unable to be either of those.

I felt I had no value.

At my diagnosis, I did feel a sense of relief—of vindication. "See! I was right. Something was wrong!" But that relief I felt didn't make up for the huge chunks of life that were now being stolen; opportunity after opportunity just out of reach. Would I ever be able to grasp that golden ring? Doubtful. Even if I could catch it,

I could not hold onto it for long. Physically speaking, the best I had been was the best I would ever be. That was a very cold, harsh reality.

But once I looked at that and acknowledged the truth of it, I began to see that the Lord saw me differently than I saw myself. I had value in His loving eyes. When I looked at myself with earthly perspective and wept, He looked with the eyes of heaven, and—although He grieved with me—He also rejoiced over my declaration when I committed that diagnosis to Him. I even went so far as to ask that He would work sanctification and holiness in my life because of it.

In spite of this perspective that God could use even this devastating disease to work His nature into me, I continuously questioned God. Was there life after MS? Who was I now? Was there any purpose to my life? Did I have value? I could not contribute anything! I was a drain on my husband, my children . . . and so on.

Choices! How could I choose to believe God, now, when He says, in Jeremiah 29:11, *"I know the plans I have for you; to prosper you and not to harm you?"* From where I stood, it no longer seemed there could be anything good left in my future.

Yet, over time, I began to understand that I have an intrinsic value that has nothing to do with what I do, or don't do. God—who loved me regardless of my performance—is who gave me that value. *"But as many as received Him, to them gave He power to become the sons of God, even to them that believe on his name" (John 1:12).* That was my true identity. When I accepted Him, I became a child of God whether I did anything else, or not. Just being His child gives me value. Jesus coming to earth to win our salvation is proof of the value God places on each of us.

But it was a long time before I could realize that truth. I had already learned my value came from what I could produce. And since I had always been able to produce, I didn't realize there was any problem with defining myself that way. Yet, those were merely social values which came from my own interpretation of family values. From working hard and having something to show for all the hard work. They also came from the society in which I grew up, that reinforced those same values.

My family had always worked hard. We had to. But we still managed to maintain a joy of life, so, I never realized there was any disagreement or disconnect between the Lord's value system and that segment of my own. However, these two value systems crashed head-on with my diagnosis. Clearly, they were not the same. I realized that determining my value by tying it to my job—and how much I produce—did not come from the Lord.

Now, I was suddenly at a crossroad, and had to choose which way I would go. Believing there was value in me without doing anything was not easy. But I still had to choose. Of course, I wanted to choose to believe the Lord, except it seemed too impossible. I didn't have the strength to choose, much less believe Him. But here is what happened. The Lord helped me make the choice to believe Him.

He did it by sending me to a potter's shop, to work with a lump of clay.

That first day, I was a novice, and the lesson was how to cut the clay from the wheel. I adjusted the wire as instructed and pushed the accelerator. I had no idea of the speed required, nor how the machine and the pot would interact. The wheel went far too fast! My pot came free, spun out of control, careened off the wheel, and landed on its head. I let out a wail—my creation lay dashed on the floor! I reached to throw it into the scrap bin thinking it beyond repair.

My instructor bounded off her stool, and scooped it up protectively. "No! No! It is not ruined. It will be beautiful! There is no such thing as a ruined pot! It is not ruined, just different. You'll see." Then she pushed, pulled, pinched, and tweaked it. It became a lovely pot—not the shape I had in mind originally—but nonetheless acceptable. I learned that I must not be firmly invested in anything I make until it comes out of the fire. Until a pot has gone through the fire, I cannot say what it is; not until it becomes what it is. I must wait and see.

From there it was no big jump to realize that when I work myself free of The Lord, I go careening off His wheel in much the same way. When I am free and think I am in control that is precisely when life spins out of control and I land on my head. Thinking life is ruined, I wail and lament. Then the loving Father scoops me up, dusts me off, pushing here and there. Pinching and tweaking, He transforms and redeems my shattered life. At times, in my distress, I cannot hear His Words of comfort when He tells me, "You are not ruined; just different than you thought you were going to be."

I was not there to give God counsel when He formed me (Psalm 139:13-18), so I do not know how far from His original design I am (Job 40:1-5). I cannot know for sure what I will be, or how I will look until I come out of the fire!

So, as I learned to control the potter's wheel much better, I was also learning to stay where the Lord put me until He moved me. Also, to do whatever task He gave me to the best of my ability—even if it was just sitting on a shelf and being a pretty pot, nurturing all who see!

My own little pots I have made grace my shelf and haven't a clue the nurture they give me. I don't have a clue the joy my company gives the Lord as I spend time sitting on His shelf, either. At times I feel banished, excluded from life, and of little value. But I am learning to recognize these as mere feelings. They are transient and have no absolute or eternal reality. Sometimes they are even the whisperings of the enemy! Then I remind myself that although I may feel banished, in reality, the Lord has scooped me up, pushed and pulled, tweaked and pinched. He has lovingly put me up out of harm's way—where I'll not be damaged—and He can enjoy His art.

My early pots do not have the precision of my later ones, but they sit next to the latest creation, and I value them no less. I have not thrown even the lumpiest of pots away. Nor has the Lord thrown me aside when, to my eyes, I am lumpy and misshapen. The cup without the handle is a pencil holder of distinction. Misshapen is unique. "Oops" became a signature mark. Ruined has become beautiful. No, I am not ruined. I am loved by my Maker.

Chronic disease can ruin me only if I take my eyes off my Maker. Chronic disease can also ruin me if I hold on too tight to the world's value system. Or, if I listen to and believe the lies of the enemy, linking value and purpose to production and dollar signs. Most importantly, I know none of those things can ruin me unless I steadfastly insist upon crawling off The Lord's wheel, or His shelf, and climbing—all by myself—into the scrap bin.

True, I am different than I was; my life is different from what I thought He planned for me. But the Lord is a good potter, who takes what life throws into the clay mix and works it into a design of beauty that I couldn't have even imagined before.

And while it is a struggle to hold on to a sense of value and meaning, that struggle is part of the tension of creation. Because I learned that, in formation, every pot is under tension—both pushed from the outside and supported from the inside. So, removed from society's hustle and bustle, I finally came to remember my original goal—the purpose behind all I have done—which was to bless the heart of my Father. Yes, what I do has changed, and even how I do it. But value and purpose? Never! Because that part came from the Lord, and not me.

That lesson at the potter's house contained several learnings for me. The first was that I must never become overly invested in what I do until it has been through the fire. Secondly, my value to God comes from being His child rather than from what I produce. Trials may change my life; they may constrain me in various ways. But they cannot define me unless I agree with the negative picture of my future, which is inherent in the trial. I must look past the trial to the hope and the future God promises in Jeremiah chapter 29, verse 11. And as I came to understand what God was teaching me, and embraced those learnings, God counted that as valuable!

 ## Ask the Holy Spirit

To make this lesson your own, identify a time, person,

project, work, or ministry in which you invested hugely but the outcome turned out to be something other than what you anticipated.

- ➢ Did it define you? Did it become "who you were?" Did it determine your value and worth?
- ➢ Did you wail and moan over your loss? Did it feel like God didn't care?
- ➢ Did you feel as though life was ruined?
- ➢ Did you try to wiggle free from the Lord's wheel by asking Him to "fix" your situation according to your guidelines?
- ➢ Ask the Holy Spirit to help you reframe that event so you can see the Master Potter's hand in it. Ask to see with the eyes of heaven what God was trying to build into you. An attitude, character trait, a skill set?
- ➢ Ask the Holy Spirit how to change your responses to your circumstances so that they will align with God's heart for you and His values.
- ➢ Ask the Holy Spirit why He wants you to make these changes.
- ➢ Ask the Holy Spirit how to implement the changes He has shown you to make.

Prayer

Thank you God for making me Your child, for giving me belonging, value and worth—help me to be able to feel it. Forgive me for believing lies about myself and my worth. Forgive me for thinking ill of You, Lord, for allowing this trial to be part of my life. I cannot see what

You see, or fully know what You have in mind for me. Grant me strength and grace, Lord, to stay on Your wheel. Today I choose to focus on what is, and can be. Help me keep that focus! I declare that You are my loving Father, and Your plans are to prosper me, to give me hope and a future!

"For I know the plans I have for you," declares the LORD, "plans to prosper you and not to harm you, plans to give you hope and a future" (Jeremiah 29:11).

Amen

On The Shelf

I've set on the shelf for some time gathering dust, or so it seems. It is the pits. Sometimes talking to God feels like an exercise in futility. What is the point? I know God is the biggest kid on the block and nothing can happen without His knowledge or permission. So why did he set me aside like this? One thing I know for sure—God is not punishing me with illness for being a bigger sinner than everyone else.

"No discipline seems pleasant at the time, but painful. Later on, however, it produces a harvest of righteousness and peace for those who have been trained by it." (Hebrews 12:11) and *"The Lord disciplines (in the sense of training rather than punishment) those he loves, as a father the son he delights in. (Proverbs 3:12)*

He either feels my being removed from life, as I have known it, is going to bring great glory to God (How? Only He knows!), or, He feels the regimen of this chronic disease will somehow develop the character and nature of Christ into my being, sooner rather than later (Again, how? Only He knows!) *"As the heavens are higher than the earth, so are my ways higher than your ways and my thoughts than your thoughts." (Isaiah 55:9)*

One thing about being on the shelf—you have time to think. I find that thinking with the "givens" of human logic leads me in circles, or to erroneous conclusions, without some intervention from the Holy Spirit. More than once I have been tempted to come to conclusions like, "God must have some sick sense of humor." Or, "There has to be some other way! God surely is not limited to use disease to create the character of Christ in a person!" Or, "You knew! You knew ahead of time and yet you allowed this to happen! What kind of a loving Father are You?" Yes, I beat on Father's chest and called His motives into question. I would exhaust myself in the endeavor and eventually become quiet. That is not good either. In the quiet I pull even more dust around myself and am tempted to pout. Or go into depression and despair. I knew that *"every good and perfect gift came down from the Father of Lights" (James 1:17)*, but it also seemed He was the one who removed those good gifts! Because surely I could not give the other guy any credit!

Then, somewhere in the mix of all that emotion, I heard from the Lord.

At the time, my husband and I were house-sitting a lovely home overlooking the ocean. I was leaning on the balcony, taking in the beauty when the Lord joined me. I learned that I was not the only one grieving over my losses, so was He. He did not want to see me damaged and disfigured. He did not want me to lose functionality. He invited me to rest in Him and to stop chasing these thoughts around in my mind. It was merely using up the precious energy I did have, and making me go in circles without coming to a resolution. Some things, He said, are beyond human comprehension. He invited me to allow Him to fight this battle for me. He assured me, yes, God would have glory from this devastation, but the how and why of that glory would not be something I could understand in this life.

In this life I do not have the capability to truly understand the value system of Heaven. Then He shared a truth I shall always hold dear. That is: Evil is incomprehensible. Evil is illogical and irrational. Evil is something so big, so huge, and so inhuman you and I cannot wrap our minds around it. You can defile your spirit by concentrating on evil, but you will never understand it. You can get a headache trying.

On the other hand, God's love and grace overcome evil. That means that God's love and grace are even more huge, powerful, illogical, and irrational, to human logic and reasoning, than evil. Therefore, you and I cannot comprehend God, either. Then the next truth: He did not create humans to comprehend Him. He created us to enjoy Him.

Okay, that helped. But I needed something else to hang on to, something smaller and more concrete. The Lord did not satisfy that need immediately, either! Instead, He gave me some powerful dreams that made it clear I was to learn the art of throwing pots on a wheel, to which I alluded in the last chapter. So, cane in hand, I hobbled down to the potter's shop, once again. I felt like Jeremiah, going down to the potter's house to hear what God had to say (Jeremiah 18:2).

There I learned that being on the shelf is as important as the form or function we are given. Once a pot is formed it sits on the shelf. Then when it becomes leather hard, it is taken back to the wheel and trimmed to its final shape. This is a time when any carving or decorating is done. Things like handles are put on, too—and then it goes back on the shelf to continue drying. It must be completely dry before it goes into the kiln, otherwise gasses within the clay might cause it to explode. Not only would it be destroyed, but any other pots around it would also be in danger. So, I saw that the drying shelf is an essential preparation for the fire.

Going into the fire prematurely causes destruction.

Having been in ministry in one form or another all of my adult life, I have heard many sad stories of people new in the faith being immediately put into offices of responsibility. That is expecting a sapling to endure a storm that only a mighty oak can survive. Which is why we need to be hidden from time to time. We need our times of discipline with a demanding coach (our time on the wheel). And we also need our times in the desert (learning hard lessons). We even need our times on the shelf to be adequately prepared for the fire of our next assignment. And we need the fire so that we can become what we were designed to be!

Looking at it in this way allows me to see that time on the shelf is not a prison sentence. It is not necessarily punishment for some sin. On the contrary, it is the Master giving honor to a vessel well formed—a vessel of value to Him.

Because He values you and me, that is His reason for putting us on the shelf!

The shelf is a time of rest, of quietness, and it's a place to learn submission and obedience. On the shelf we have the time to develop depth of relationship with Him. When I am quiet I can hear what He is teaching me. As I submit, my thoughts no longer take me into murky areas of doubt about God's character or motives. And as the messages of doubt are stilled, I can better concentrate to focus on the picture or lesson He is giving me. I can even see new avenues open up to me that I could not see before in all the other noise, busyness, and confusion.

I might even go so far as to say the way becomes much clearer as I give up the endeavor of trying to use my human understanding. Yes, there are many losses in life; that is truth. But, I have confidence that at some point, perspective on those losses will come.

The important thing is, I'm no longer trying to work myself off the shelf to get back into life. There is life on the shelf! My wiggling off the shelf would simply result in falling on my head, again, and then I would have to go back to the beginning and start over. It would cost the Master precious time. Not to mention that much later down the line; I would still end up on the shelf—again!

So, little by little I begin to see that it is better for me to stay here until the Master sees I am ready for the fire! He has invested His Son's life in me. He has no desire that I explode. Now, I know I will come off the shelf when He says I am ready. Until then I occupy myself with things that will fill this fragile vessel of mine with His nature and character, rather than destroy it.

Ask the Holy Spirit

I would encourage those of you who find yourselves still on the dung heap, who keep Job company, to have confidence that God is able to not only withstand your emotions, but to actually bring order to the emotional chaos you may feel. But He cannot create emotional order for us if we do not share the chaos with Him. I find journaling or writing letters to God helps bring the emotion out of my head or heart and onto the page so that I can see exactly what it is I feel.

You can trust Him with your upside-down-and-sideways-to-the-world emotions. Tell Him everything. Then rest in His arms, wait and listen for His heart, and His words of comfort and assurance. He will never leave you or abandon you.

- Write so that you know what you feel. Then write out the Lord's response to your emotional spring cleaning
- If you are having trouble thanking God for your time in the wilderness (or your time on the shelf), ask Him to show you what is preventing your thankfulness.
- Ask Him to reveal the aspect(s) of His nature and character that He and you are working on. The emotions the difficulties of the wilderness, and shelf time cause to rise to the surface can easily bury God's purposes in our lives. We need occasional reminders!
- Ask Him to increase your capacity to hold His wisdom and values.
- Ask the Holy Spirit to show you ways you sulk and pout, so you can make more immediate efforts to get over them. Because they have the same effect as humidity on clay. It makes the clay

retain moisture so it takes longer to become dry enough for the fire. Sulking, pouting, and resisting all extend the time on the shelf.
- ➤ Ask for the most strategic way to become what you are designed to be. Commit to lean into it.
- ➤ Ask Him what keeps you from basking in the joy and light of the Son. Sonshine dries you out and readies you for the fire so that you are no longer potential; you become your potential in reality. It is manifested in your life!

Prayer

Father God, I have a limited perspective, I admit that. Draw me close. Still the chatter in my mind and the clamor of my emotions so that I can hear Your heart. Help me submit to the discipline of rest—not as punishment but as training in obedience and self-control. I thank you for what you are building into me even though I do not fully comprehend what that is or what I will look like when you finish. Anoint me with patience and touch my eyes so that I can see the treasure of this time. Expand me Father. Enlarge my capacity to see and contain more of you; lift me up so I might see from your perspective. Thank you for delighting in me and valuing me so much that you have put me up here on the shelf and out of harm's way as you lovingly prepare me for my next assignment.

"This is what the Sovereign Lord, the Holy One of Israel, says: "In repentance and rest is your salvation, in quietness and trust is your strength, but you would have none of it." (Isaiah 30:15)

Amen

The Trouble With Centering

I always use a cane when walking; I list hard to the right. When I rise out of a chair I must do so in stages, and then stand still for a moment to allow the world to stop moving. I started moving too quickly once, in an effort to answer the phone. I lost balance; over I went, and tore up my knee. I missed that phone call.

I appreciate well-placed furniture and handrails.

With the MS there is an inability to lift my feet; so I shuffle rather than walk, and I have a mild numbness in my feet. Uneven ground requires that I take someone's arm. In addition to lack of mobility, flexibility is also diminished. Walking takes great effort. It feels as if I were in some kind of harness and pushing against a thick, wide rubber band. It is exhausting! Sometime during 2004, nine years after the attack, I learned that connective tissue will thicken to help support a traumatized area. The sense of pushing against a broad, thick band was more accurate than I knew!

The attack of MS shook me to the core. I became dependent on my husband and God in ways that I had never been before, and I was not sure it was a safe place to be. I pulled back, deep within myself. In my eyes I had lost physical attractiveness, and my mental abilities were impaired.

I had a hard time believing anyone would choose or value me. I had little confidence in people's staying power, and I was not even sure if God would stay around for more than a block. As perspective returned, I was able to see that He's been here since time began. Still, it is hard when we do not always feel His presence or see Him in the details of life. For a long time, fear and insecurity had me by both ears and were speaking louder than my Lord's voice. I was living on rocky, uneven ground. In one sense, needing a steady arm to lean on is a good thing—that way I will always stay close to God! He is the one who gives faith, and *"...faith is the substance of things hoped for, the evidence of things not seen." (Hebrews 11:1)*.

During my post-MS quest for purpose, value, and meaning in life, the Lord sent two powerful dreams making it quite clear that questions I had yet to ask would be answered as I worked with clay. On the way to my lessons in clay, I remembered an Old Testament prophet had also been sent to the potter's house to learn a thing or two from the Lord (Jeremiah 18:1-2). I thought, "Hmmm, this is going to be interesting, a living parable—I will see what the Lord is teaching me as I am doing it. I will find the answers to unformed questions; I will find both the answers and the questions in the clay." Believe me; I had plenty of questions for The Almighty!

Basic to any work on a potter's wheel is the centering of the clay. The lump must be in the very center of the wheel, otherwise the pot will be out of balance and the forming and trimming of the pot will be more difficult—not impossible, just more difficult. Clay that is not centered wobbles and is limited in the height to which it can go.

The wobble develops as the forming pot reaches a point of critical mass. (When you are in the middle of your hard place, it feels like critical mess!) Skilled potters are able to re-center the clay by bringing it back down into a less-formed state and taking out the air bubble, or the wobble, with what is called a "left hand compression." If one is not skilled enough to do the compression, when the pot wobbles it is time to stop and call it a pot! If a potter continues to work as it wobbles, a chunk will separate itself off at the point at which the clay is off center.

Once you have called it a pot, and cut it loose from the wheel, it goes to the drying shelf. When a pot becomes leather hard the excess is trimmed off—everything that is not the pot is cut away. This is the final shaping. To trim this excess, the pot must again be centered on the wheel. For an off-center, out-of-balance pot, obtaining this second centering is a difficult process. It is quite likely that the trimming will also be somewhat off center. The wall on one side will be thicker than the wall on the other side. It is likely that the trimming tool will take more of a bite out of one side of the pot than the other, so it may list to one side.

So what does this have to do with finding value and purpose when one's life is in a shattered heap? The Lord kept drawing my attention to the fact that I have trouble centering. Suddenly it clicked in my mind that I was already in the parable and I should pay close attention. Just as I was having trouble physically centering the clay, so spiritually I was having trouble staying centered in Jesus and resting in Him. Looking at my off-center pot, it was obvious to me that if I was not centered, then all of my life would be out of balance.

Further, if I successfully trimmed an off-balance pot and sent it into the fire, it would be out of balance for the rest of its existence. Hmmm, I didn't like that implication! I didn't think I wanted to be permanently out of balance with no possibility for repairing that state! So, I redoubled my efforts to center and be centered.

Finally, I became frustrated because most of my pots were still just a little off. I believe the Lord allowed this to happen so that I could see with my own eyes the results of being out of balance:

1. I am in danger of losing chunks of potential.
2. I am limiting myself in capacity in whatever I do.
3. As the Lord trims from my life that which is not a part of His design, His tools may take larger bites than He would like, leaving me less than well rounded.
4. I run the risk of breaking in the process.

My goal has never been to be broken, to be of little or no use to my Savior. Spiritually speaking, lack of balance means I may have thick protective walls around some areas of my life, but in other areas the protection is thin or non-existent, so that I am vulnerable on many different levels.

God made it painfully clear that I must pay the price of submission in the natural as well as the spiritual realm. I struggled and struggled with centering the clay by myself. I didn't want to pay for more instruction! Surely, I should be able to do this myself! Well, it seems, I surely could not! Sometimes one lesson is not enough; we need to ask for help, and pay for additional instruction.

Spiritual currency is far more costly than any money I will pay for instruction. Spiritually, I pay with spiritual pride. I pay with bites taken from my self-confidence, independence, and self-sufficiency. I pay with the surrender of my homemade self-image. This currency is far dearer than money. Giving up pride, confidence in self, and independence says that I have come to a place where I say, "I can't do this myself, God, please do it in me, for me."

When I was a child I raised my arms and my father picked me up and put me where I needed to be. After so many years of walking with God am I still so immature that I need him to pick me up and put me where I need to be? What a blow to "mature" adult pride, to self-confidence and self-sufficiency! Expensive on one hand, but the alternative is even more costly.

There is a point at which clay cannot be worked anymore.

It can only tolerate being drawn up, pushed back down and pushed around so much, and then it just collapses in on itself and cannot keep its shape. It must then be kneaded to remove air bubbles and excess water, then formed again into a ball or thrown back into the bin, worked into other clay, and allowed to start over. It is not thrown away, but much time and energy has been lost. Scripture says there is a point at which God will no longer contend with a man or a woman (Genesis 6:3). At some point He will end the forming process and will allow us to be what we will be.

A sign in the pottery studio where I work says, "It is time to call it a pot." I do not want to be thrown back into the bin to start over. Nor do I want to go through the fire and have limited capacity, lack of function, or inferior design baked in as permanent parts of my life. I really do want to be a vessel fit for the King's table! Looking deeper than the surface, the Lord saw my desire to be holy and devoted to Him. It seems, however, that I want to call myself a pot before I am fully formed!

When I form a bowl, a cup, or a vase, they look much the same for a time. For a goodly portion of the formation process I can change my mind about which vessel a given lump will become. Before the MS attack I thought I knew the design of my life. Now I realize the Lord's work in me was far from finished! My life had not yet reached the time to make those decisive strokes of formation. Indeed, only God knows when I will reach that point! Until then He may change me any number of times, in any number of ways. I believe that by submitting to the pressure of the Master's hand, He can not only take the wobble out of my life, but he can also form me into a holy vessel of great beauty as well as function.

The test of centered clay is that it appears to be standing still while whirling around at incredible speed. As I am centered in Him, life can literally be whirling round me and I can be at rest. At rest in Him, I can tolerate the centrifugal force of life, but if I am out of balance it will tear me apart. My life before MS was a whirl. Through this parable I hear Him calling me away from the whirl into the center, to rest in Him. To get there, I must submit, I must stop struggling to return to the whirl. I must offer up to Him all that the whirl means to me—what it says to me about meaning and value.

I struggled and struggled to come to rest in Him as if

I could do it on my own. What an oxymoron! How could I, by my own effort come to rest in Him! He must bring me to center. I must submit to the Master Potter again, and again.

So, I put out the money and my instructor put her hands over mine and said, "Like this. It needs to feel this way. Just a little more pressure . . . here." As I submitted to the pressure of my instructor's hands, I also realized I must submit to the Master Potter's hand in my life and not fight the pressure of that hand, lest I develop a nasty wobble and risk becoming an inferior sample of His work.

I did it. I paid the fee. I received the instruction. And the first thing I discovered was that the clay was stuck. I knew that. But now I had eyes to see! For a time I stared, allowing the impact of it to settle deep within me. Clay cannot move itself to center regardless of how sincerely it may desire to do so. Wow! Knowing was now in my heart, not just my head, and in that moment I knew that I am to thank God whenever I am stuck spiritually—going nowhere! When I take the condemnation out of being stuck it simply indicates that I am in a position where the Master can put His hand into my life and bring me to center.

I was the one who said, "Surely, I can do this." I learned that surely, I could not.

All I could do was invite the Lord to bring me to rest in Him. All I could do was set my heart to allow His pressure in my life without resisting. I could still be real about my emotions. I could tell Him honestly what hurt and that I did not enjoy some aspect of the process—that I would rather be fishing! I could say all these things and still retain the set of my heart. Just because I didn't like something didn't mean I wouldn't go through with it—like having a root canal!

The next thing I discovered was that the clay did not submit easily. It fights the hand that forms it, even if it should sincerely want to be submissive. There are bumps in some places of the lump and dips in others, but in the centering process these are evened out. Sort of like, *"Every valley shall be filled in, every mountain and hill made low . . . the rough ways smooth" (Luke 3:5).*

My instructor cupped her hand around the clay, braced her elbow into her body, and leaned into the clay with the full force of her body. Her hand applied pressure at three key places:

1. The juncture of the pinky finger and the hand pressed the base, or foundation

2. The juncture of the index finger and the hand pressed the middle

3. The thumb went over the top to keep it from squirting up in an undisciplined fashion

The Master literally hems me in! Should the clay squirt up, and come out the top of the hand, it would torque, or twist, all the way to its base. In the process of bringing me to center, the Master may apply pressure to my foundations—I may have to look at old stuff. I may need to clean up unresolved issues I thought I had carefully tucked away and shut the lid on. God has a way of looking right into the heart of dusty old issues. He does not forget items I retire to the "archives" and conveniently forget. Such unresolved problems create air bubbles, pockets that cause wobbles later in life for which the cause is difficult to discern. More importantly, they obscure The Glory within!

At times, the balance problem lays in current circumstances. Pressure at this point feels like all hell breaking loose. I like things to be neat and organized but when pressures hem me in on all sides, life is no longer neat. I lose the ability to control and organize. It is easy at such times to forget what I know, to become confused in my thinking, and to lose sight of my options. When life goes out of control, that is when I forget who I am, and Who is on The Throne.

Slowly, I began to discover that being under God's thumb is not necessarily a result of sin. Sometimes it is because He loves me so much He does not want to risk losing me. He wants to bring out of me some treasure He hid in there that I would not find in easier circumstances. Sometimes He puts His thumb over my life (or in my life) to keep me well rounded—to keep my life from becoming twisted. I saw a pot that had been fired from a ball of clay that was torqued to the base. That pot was one twisted sister! The firing had made the twists even more obvious. It was of no use at all except as an example of what happens to improperly centered clay!

Spiritually speaking, I tend to protest when the Lord leans on me. When I am under his thumb I moan and groan, kvetch, and carry on. Sometimes I fight the Lord's hand like that lumpy bumpy piece of clay. But in the end, I weary of the struggle and yield just like the clay. I don't really want anything other than His will—I am just afraid of what will happen to me, or where it will take me. I don't understand what He is doing, or why. I don't see the beginning from the end. I can't see what He has in mind, or the design He is creating in me. I probably wouldn't comprehend what I was looking at even if I could see it!

I like comfort and safety. Stretching can be painful. I like things predictable. Limits and boundaries are good. But sometimes potters dig their thumbs into the border (or boundary) to give the pot a pour spout, or to make a prettier border. While painful, it is worth it in the end.

I say, "I want to be free." I hear others say it. "I want to be free of addiction, co-dependency, old habits, old ways, etc." When I set my pot free, I took a long, thin piano wire and cut the pot from the wheel. Even being freed requires a cutting away! In a couple days the pot will be leather hard and I will, once again, run that wire underneath. Some of the thin film that was left on the working platform will remain on the platform, but some will stick to the pot and have to be removed with another sharp implement even before I can trim.

The entire process of the formation of a vessel fit for use is one of pressure, pulling, pushing and cutting away anything that is not part of the image of the vessel in the mind of the potter. And then, the heat...the fire! Any vessel of beauty—not just function, but beauty, will have to face the fire at the very least twice. Some of the most beautiful and valuable endure the heat a dozen times or more.

Firing is a tricky thing. The pot must be completely bone dry before it faces the fire otherwise gas can build up and cause an explosion. The danger in an explosion is that the shards may damage some or all of the other pots in the kiln—expensive! The same happens to us when we are put into leadership or ministry positions before we are "cured"—healed and properly supported from the inside and the outside. We must be prepared for the tension involved in the pushing, pulling of spiritual and natural forces that come to bear in relationships between people who are also in the formation and firing processes.

Right now, I feel very humble and quite submissive. I'm almost ready to sing that song, "You are the potter, I am the clay. Mold me, make me. Fill me, use me." But, you see; now I have a much fuller understanding of what is involved! If I do sing that song, I know the Lord will take me seriously. My hopes and my prayers are these:

That when I feel myself under the Lord's thumb, when I feel His pressure in my life, or the bite of his trimming, that I can remember what I know.

That I will be able to thank Him for the time and trouble He takes to bring me to center, for the care He takes in shaping His purposes in my life.

That I can thank Him for persevering when I fight His hand in my life.

That I can thank Him for His design for my life.

That I can thank Him for seeing beyond this lump to the value and purpose of my life even when I can't, and cherishing it.

That I can remember who I am and Who He is.

And finally—in spite of how painful life may be or become—that I can feel His love and care for this one stubborn, wobbly pot!

 ## Ask the Holy Spirit

Submission is the key! When God indicates an issue, go there whether it is foundational or in present day life! Repent, give, and receive forgiveness, understanding, and comfort—whatever the Lord brings to you. When He puts His thumb in your life and leans on you it's because He loves you. When He wants to excise some rotten carnal flesh, hold still and allow Him to do so. The end result is great beauty and glory to God. When you develop a wobble in life, be as gracious as possible while He does a "left handed compression." Pay the price—the result is worth it!

- Identify where the Lord is applying pressure in your life.
- At your foundations (old baggage that has not been dealt with).
- In your here and now (it feels like all hell breaking loose).
- Where He has His thumb in or over your life, lovingly hemming you in so that you can become spiritually well rounded.
- What aspect of His character is He building in you?
- Where are you stuck?
- Where is life out of balance? Ask Him to show you what change you need to make that is strategic at this time.
- Ask Him to show you how to change and how to implement that change.
- What are the lies you have believed about yourself and about God, and what is the spiritual currency with which He requires of you for instruction?
- What is the Lord cutting away at this time?

Prayer

Thank you God for loving me even before the

foundation of the world was established. You had great joy in writing the book that is my life, designing it chapter by chapter. I am glad that you know the end from the beginning, because for me, right now, it is confusing, hard, and painful. But You have shown me Your character which never changes and which is that You are a loving father. You will work all things for my good. So in these times of being formed, I hold onto Your character and thank you for loving and caring enough to put up with my wailing. My heart is to be a holy vessel that can grace Your banqueting table so please do not stop forming me regardless of the noise I make in the process! Grant me strength and grace, Lord, to stay with Your process so that I will be equipped and ready for the fire of the next assignment.

I declare that You are my loving Father, and Your plans are good!

"Before I formed you in the womb I knew you, before you were born I set you apart; I appointed you...." (Jeremiah 1:5)

Amen

On Brokenness

At the end of 1997 I hit a wall. I found myself unable to do the things I needed to do. My health had improved —I was light years ahead of where I had been right after the MS attack in Dec.'95—and I was even able to travel with my husband, who was teaching. During that time, I met some folks who were working with a deaf community. At that point, I knew that life as I had known it was over, and I was asking God what life looked like after MS. Who was I, and where did I fit? Could my life still have meaning or purpose?

This deaf community wanted material that my husband was teaching in a format they could use. They needed a translation that I could do with my limited physical resources. Since I needed to find some meaning for my life, I plunged in, grateful to have some purpose. I completed the first draft of the curriculum, as well as a first draft of *The Mystery of Spiritual Sensitivity*, and then I hit this wall. I wanted to finish both projects but could not move myself to do so. I cared about them a great deal, but all I could do was knit.

I had found a group of women who knitted and crocheted blankets for the needy in the city where we lived, and I started knitting. Anything more than handwork was too much. The emotional state I was in was just short of curling up into the fetal position. I knew I was not depressed. I had been there, and this was not depression. I could think, relate, talk, pray, care, but I could not do much of anything. Oh, sometimes I would twist my own arm and accomplish some things, but I quickly exhausted myself. Dusting the windowsills and watering my violets was a day's work!

David and I have a psychologist friend who sends us things to read periodically. One of the articles he sent at that time contained a comment about motivation coming from the soul. That rolled around in me for a couple days and prompted me to write back, "Can we have a broken soul? I know we can have a broken spirit, but what about the soul?"

His response was, "Yes!" And it was such a strong yes that it even surprised him. He recounted a brief case study of a recent client's story—my song, second verse. Then he told me how he had come to be broken in one area of his own life. He said it was like having a broken neck. You can want to get up and move. You can command your body to do so, but nothing happens. He said that need could look him in the eye but he could not do anything about it. People could scold, push, make him feel guilty, but he simply could not do anything about it. It was not for lack of caring. He cared a great deal, and it hurt him not to be able to respond. And, like me, he could twist his own arm and make himself act, but quickly came to the end of himself.

He went on to say that for some reason it seems very important to God that we know we are broken. It also seems very important to God that the world knows we are broken. He thought it had something to do with "holding this mystery in earthen vessels—and earthen vessels break very easily."

Once again, like Jeremiah (Jeremiah 18:2), God sent me back to the potter's house. This time, I learned that there are different types of clay. There, surrounded by the musty earthen smell, it was God, me, a ball of clay. and a whirring wheel. There the Lord reminded me of some things.

A potter chooses the type of clay based somewhat on the purpose of the vessel. Each has its own tensile strength, its limitations—something of its own personality. Within the limitations of the clay, creativity can abound! If the limitations are exceeded, the vessel will either be lost or have to be trimmed down or compressed down and reformed. Should terra cotta aspire to be porcelain, or vice versa, that vessel would be writing a formula for frustration and would likely end up broken. Porcelain can never be terra cotta and terra cotta can never be porcelain.

Terra cotta is tough stuff; it can take a lot of weight, a lot of hard use. When on the potter's wheel, a great deal of pushing and shoving is needed to center it.

Montana Grey is much easier to center on the wheel but you have to be careful. It is easier to work with because it contains "groog"—little particles which make it more malleable, but which can also cut and slice your hand! Then there is porcelain—fragile stuff. The artist has to have the right touch.

I looked up to heaven and shook my head. "Yeah, kind of like us! Some of us require a lot of pushing and shoving to convince us to be in the center of Your will and in the process we may take a slice of the very hand that forms us. Other times we become fragile and fall apart. Gosh, Lord, what You have to work with!"

My friend had confirmed my sense of brokenness; I grieved for two days. After my two days of weeping, I toddled over to the computer: "Computer, give me everything you have on break, broke, broken, brokenhearted, etc.—I want all the verses with any form of the word "break." The computer responded and the printer served me up a large stack of 8 ½ x 11 pages! Then I went to my husband's Greek and Hebrew tomes.

A picture began to form in my mind. There are two kinds of breaking: the kind God does and the kind the Enemy does. The kind God does may hurt like anything but it results in beauty of character and strength of spirit. The kind the enemy designs is for our destruction.

And that was the kind I was experiencing.

There are two types of this destructive breaking. The first is to grab a person or a pot and dash it to pieces suddenly (a drunk driver comes across the median and you wake up a paraplegic or quadriplegic; or someone you trust betrays you—that sort of thing—a "suddenly"). The second is to be weighed down and weighed down and weighed down by the cares of life so that you bend and bend and bend until you break—like a tree limb in an ice storm. The freezing rain slowly adds weight as the ice builds, until, finally, the limb breaks.

One of the references for breaking that is of the "dashed to pieces" kind, is found in Job 17:1. *"My days have passed. All my plans and dreams are shattered (dashed to pieces suddenly)."* That caught up my feelings. It seemed that all The Lord had called me to, all I had planned to do and dreamed of doing was shattered to pieces. I crawled up on the dung heap with Job to contemplate this state of affairs and to try to find some sense in it, some logic, some meaning, maybe some of the why of it. At this time I had no clue that the decisions I made while in this state were parts of a life test and would, or would not be, credited to me as something valuable. That understanding would not come for another fourteen years!

On life's dung heap The Lord began to speak to me with pictures, thoughts, and by tweaking my memory. He first showed me a picture of myself standing in a puddle. I knew with the knowing that comes with dreams and visions that the puddle on the floor was my life juice. I was like a car with a hole in the transmission line. The fluid drained out and that car was not going anywhere. I looked at the puddle with no emotion. My mind said, "That is your life juice there. You should be alarmed. This is not good." And I answered myself, "Oh, yeah. Yup. It's not good. Oh, well."

Then He reminded me of a beautifully hand painted, gold-rimmed china bowl I inherited from my grandmother. I thought, "Boy, if some jerk came into my house and accidentally or on purpose, smashed that bowl I would not throw it out. I would gently pick up the pieces and lovingly glue them back together again. Then, even if some little piece was missing, I would not put the bowl out of sight, but on a shelf. It is precious to me, not for what it could do, but because of who it is from. I would keep the bowl because I love and honor my grandmother. Even though it could never be used again in the manner for which it was designed, I would put it in a place of honor where everyone who came to my house could see it. I would make a point of saying, "See! This is my inheritance! Isn't it beautiful?" Decorating my shelf would become its new function. I said, "Well, Lord, I am your inheritance and I am broken. This is what I would do with my inheritance. What would You do?"

Jesus interrupted my reverie, reminding me of His mandate in Isaiah 60:1 to "bind up" the broken hearted. Ugh, now I had to move and do some more word study! I dragged out the big Strong's concordance and found the word for heart (leeb)—it includes the will, the emotions, and the intellect. From reading my husbands reference books that said "soul" to me. It looked like the Hebrew talk about the heart, and the Greeks about the soul, but they mean essentially the same thing. So if Jesus came to bind up the broken hearted or broken souls, it felt like another confirmation of the brokenness of soul that I was experiencing. "But binding up, Lord—what about that?"

The word translated "bind up" means to wrap tightly like a turban or a compress. That flashed me back to the picture of the puddle on the floor. I said, "Yes, Lord! A compress would stop the bleeding!" It was obvious from the scripture that the binding up process was the Lord's job. There was to be no self-help here—no "ten easy steps" to bind one's self up. Well, maybe they exist, but that would be man's ideas rather than God's prescription!

I sat back in my prayer chair meditating on what He had shown me, but the attitude of my spirit was that of standing with arms raised waiting for Father to reach down with a big swatch of gauze to bind me up. With the patio door open I could hear the dull roar of the surf and the seagulls calling overhead. Cars came and went; people busy about their lives. The window sheers billowed with a breeze heavy with the smell of salt and seaweed. Life was going on as usual, as if nothing was wrong, while my life juices slowly drained into that puddle and I waited for God to bind me up.

The phone ringing brought me out of my meditation. It was an invitation to an award ceremony. Elijah House Ministries wanted to honor me for work I had done which continues to have ongoing effects around the world. I had just asked the Lord how He would bind me up and the call came! It was as if the Lord was saying, "This is how I will bind you up, by honoring you. You see, Carol, you are not wrong about the bowl. That is what I would do too! You are broken, but you are my inheritance and I will not throw you away. I will lift you up to a place of honor and I will say to all who come to Me, 'See! She's my inheritance! Isn't she great! Isn't she beautiful?"

I was overcome with the specific detail of the Lord's planning. Each of us is so unique and yet He finds a way to bind up His broken ones that is unique to each one and to the kind of brokenness they have experienced. The sense of being loved, chosen and honored by my Father was complete and total. For the first time in years I had a sense that in whatsoever circumstance I would find myself, I could be content—really content. I said, "Lord, if You do not heal me this side of heaven, and if I never produce anything again, if I am never any more than just a pretty pot on Your shelf, it is enough. It is enough!"

Obviously, the Lord did not leave me on the shelf with

nothing to do, but to be safe in future assignments He has for me, I had to come to the place of being willing to be simply a decoration.

Jesus said to stop sinning (John 8:11b). He would not have needed to teach repentance if there was no sin. In the book of James, He admonishes us to confess our sins to one another (James 5:16). Although there is a large spiritual component to the MS attack, I also have a part in my present dilemma. To explain that I need to tell you that when I was a youngster, my father told me if I worked hard, I could do whatever I put my mind to.

Of course, we lived on a farm and my father had no idea that I would ever work too hard. The limits of the seasons and of daylight and dark were natural boundaries for my farmer father. Times of rest and refreshment were built into that rural rhythm. But I grew up and went off to university, marriage, and a career where there were lights, lights, and more lights. No one ever told me my body had limits, so I forced it to keep up with my mind. Without realizing, I took on more than I should have. With my earthly father's words ringing in my ears, why would I think to limit myself? I did not know the properties of the clay from which I was made. I did not take the time to ask my heavenly Father, either, so I exceeded my design capabilities and like a clay pot, I am now broken. I went at life as if I were terra cotta and found that I contain more porcelain than I knew.

I have learned that stress and over work is a formula for bringing dormant MS to the surface. It is possible that I could have avoided this last attack if I had listened to the tugs of the Holy Spirit to rest. But the vision was so large ... the need so great! It never occurred to me that He who gave the vision also commits to finish what He starts (Philippians 1:6). I had not realized that I was doing spiritual work with the strength of my soul—using my will to push my body instead of the wisdom of the Holy Spirit who knows our frame and when we need to slow down or stop to rest. I went beyond the design capabilities of my body and soul—and I broke! I felt a great kinship to Job and went back on the dung heap with him.

And, like Job, I questioned God. Like Job, I did not receive an answer to my, "Why?" At least I didn't get an answer that I understood. However, God met the emotional cry of my heart with the assurance of His love, and He began the restoration.

I still had a problem with motivation. Then I heard a message that spurred me to dig for a word meaning, again. Something in this message made me think that motivation may be tied to vision in some way. I looked up vision and found all sorts of interesting words derived from the root word.

Vision is part of the word pro-"vision" in English! Although the "seeing" part has fallen out of the meaning in current usage, at one time that was part of the meaning of our present day English word. When vision is lost, does motivation go with it? According to my psychologist friend Dr. Jim, the answer to that question is "No," because motivation is necessary to have vision in the first place. However, when our dreams, our pictures of ourselves and what we are or will be doing in the future are lost, all too often the sense of identity is also lost. I don't mean dreams from sleep, but rather a visualizing of a future for yourself—plans or deep, strong desires about what you want to do, or be. If we wrap ourselves up in this sort of vision—this picture that we form for ourselves—then if life goes sideways and we see the "dream" lost, we lose sight of who we are and where we fit. We no longer have the motivation to make a dream happen because it is lost to us, no longer possible to attain. But if our sense of self is anchored firmly in God's character, and the work done by Jesus, then we are not at risk for losing our "self" when storms rage or the earth moves under us. Even though when the hard things of life happen, it may take us some time to get back to this place of solid foundation. From this place we build a new "vision"—a new dream that comes from God rather then from our own minds, and with it comes hope and motivation.

Hebrews 11:1 says, *"Faith is the substance of things hoped for, the evidence of things not seen."* Faith is a complex thing. It means to believe in things we cannot see and believing in things that are true. You cannot see gravity, but you believe in the law of gravity because you see the evidence of it. Faith is a raw material God uses to create the things we envision that are aligned with His will for us. Seeing that picture God gives of our future, even though it is not physically present, brings joy, and joy creates the energy for motivation to press toward that goal. A sense of purpose comes with having a vision for your life.

But, *"Where there is no vision, (no picture of our future) the people perish: but he that keepeth the law, happy is he. (Proverbs 29:18)*. Faith, when it is called "the evidence of things not seen," means that when a person acts in faith, she gives testimony to her belief in the existence and power of a God that no one can see. When a woman goes to her death praising God, her faith is evidence that she believes we have a powerful God. *"...for by it the elders obtained a good report,"* Hebrews says. And *"...before Jesus translation, he had this testimony, that he pleased God."* By faith we act and we give evidence to the reality of God, his character, and we also give evidence to our belief in him.

I believe that Satan, being aware of the destiny God decreed for me, made an all out assault to eliminate me. I also believe that just as he was not allowed to take Job's life, he was not allowed to take mine. God graciously gave me something to do, then slowly, as I engaged Him in the process of doing "the one thing" He would tell me to do, a level of joy returned and I slowly began to have the energy to support a small amount of motivation.

He helped me learn how to steward my little bit—it became my widow's mite, the last bit of flour and oil made into a cake and given to Elijah, my alabaster jar. I'm sure Mary had no idea that she was anointing Jesus for burial as she wept, wiped his feet with her hair, and poured out her perfume on him. Some sixteen years after diagnosis He finally shared this perspective of building value into me by developing in me Jesus' nature and character, but while in the thick of the process I did not have that perspective.

These lessons were difficult and painful. It has not been easy to be patient when locked up inside my body, year after year, because of a seemingly random and meaningless attack. Now, looking at the disease from the perspective of it being the means by which value can be accomplished in me, it is much easier for me to work with, rather than see it as an enemy to be fought against and conquered! I no longer want to cut the process short. I want my life to be infused with all the value I can contain!

 ## Ask the Holy Spirit

There is an abundance of wisdom in the admonition, "Know yourself!" The following will help you to know yourself as you log your responses.

- What are the things that present limits in your life?
- Are these limitations, or boundaries that you and the Lord developed together?
- Ask the Lord if you are exceeding His boundaries for you.
- Ask Him if you are doing the work of the spirit with the strength of the soul, i.e. by your own will power, force of your own personality, and strength of conviction that what you are doing is the right thing to do.
- Ask the Lord to show you the type of clay from which you are made and what the inherent limitations of that clay are. What are its strengths and weaknesses?
- Ask Him to show you where and when you are to stop. This will help you adjust your boundaries! He knows what you are made of, and for. He never asks terra cotta to perform the tasks of porcelain, and vice-versa. He who gives the vision will also complete it.
- If you have lost your motivation, was your identity

coming from the "vision" or from God? Look for what has happened. What happened to your joy, the source of your energy?
- ➢ What was the event that damaged your dream and your ability to envision? Do you have a vision or dream for your life?
- ➢ Ask the Lord to show you the changes you need to make so that you can see the new vision He has for you.

Prayer

Thank you God for Your word.

I confess Father, that I am broken and I've lost my sense of who I am; I have no motivation for anything. Please come find me in my lostness, bind up my broken places, and restore me. Show me what You see. Tell me who I am, in You, and once again may I know the joy of having a vision of a hope and a future. I praise You. You are a good God. My head knows this to be true regardless of what my emotions may say. Hang onto me hanging on to You.

"My frame was not hidden from you when I was made in the secret place, when I was woven together in the depths of the earth." (Psalm 139:15)

Amen.

Part Two
THE VISIONS

Regaining My Balance

The MS attack had catapulted me into a wilderness of fear and insecurity. One might think it would make me give up on trying to do things for myself, but in my case it had the opposite effect. The more fearful I felt, the more I tried to control my own life. And since I'm a nurturer, I also tried to control the lives of the people around me.

Slowly, the Lord began to show me that I had become attached, or harnessed, to responsibility. Being the responsible one had become my identity—that is who I was. But my nature is to nurture; I cannot not nurture! It is who I am, and in that, I am in His likeness. Yes, but when nurture is given in the flesh—from my own personal emotional reservoir rather than from His divine nature, through the agency of His Holy Spirit—that equates to doing spiritual work with the strength of the soul, rather than the strength of The Spirit. It is akin to running on battery power when we could be plugging into God! Nurture out of the flesh becomes responsibility, then duty, and after awhile I lose the joy nurturing should give.

My creative, analytical mind would automatically tend to see further steps or ways to shore up and strengthen someone else. Because I could see how to do it, and the benefit it would bring, I would also tend to feel responsible to make it happen. Which is a knee-jerk reaction and often leads to a lack of inner balance. But if I was to turn what I saw into a prayer, and invite Jesus into the situation, He would partner with me and take the responsibility on Himself. He showed me how the prayer is a way of leaning on Him and using His strength to make things happen, rather than my own. He would show me the bits I can do without causing myself harm. He would also show me the bits that are for someone else to do, as well as the bits that God, Himself, wants to carry. He maintains the balance!

The cure for my over-responsibility was to learn to talk to God about what I saw before taking up an intercession into someone else's life. He may not want me to take on a particular responsibility or a particular burden. He may give it to someone else, or take it on Himself! He wanted me to learn to nurture through His strength, so that I could experience His joy of how nurture builds other people. They will respond with health, and joy. If I nurture through Him rather than through my own strength, my spirit will benefit from His joy, as well as theirs.

It was wonderful to discover that I could bring delight to the hearts of God's people by doing what I do best. It created something in my spirit akin to dancing in the spirit. And to see other people's spirits leap within them, tickles me. It tickles them, too, to see how much I enjoy them. That is something that pleases and delights our Father. Our mutual delight creates a three-way flow of joy that leads people into wholeness. He showed me there was also a way for me to successfully use what I am good at—to teach and relate, to communicate truth—even if what I was communicating was something difficult. People do not mind facing something difficult with me when those things are presented in an environment of acceptance. Nurturing through Him, in this way, will no longer feel like responsibility or work, and will not drain my energies.

I could do this in spite of MS!

But in order to move into these new assignments He had for me, the Lord first led me to address my own fears and insecurities—to go to the roots—before we could move on. I had to allow Him to dig up the spiritual soil around my roots and remove the things that were decreasing fruitfulness and hindering my ability to receive nurture from Him.

To know He has plans for me, regardless of the MS, gave me new strength. I may be a bruised reed, but those are the ones to whom He gives a great deal of loving attention. I am the reed pipe He inherited from His Father upon which He could still create beautiful music.

 ## Ask the Holy Spirit

God also has plans for you. No matter what you're suffering through, you can count on this truth: God is working in you, to bring you closer to him, so that you can be more effective at whatever task he gives you.

> ➤ Am I out of balance in my walk with You?

- What do I need to hold onto to be balanced and grounded?
- What exercise will develop the spiritual mobility and flexibility characteristic of a healthy strong spirit and bring You joy?
- What is holding me back in my walk with Jesus?
- What am I harnessed to? What is the harness?
- What discipline do I need, in order to improve my relationship with Jesus?

Prayer

Thank you, Jesus for loving me and caring enough that You came to earth and lived among us. You know how we suffer. You were able to keep in balance, listening to Your Father and yet able to relate in healthy ways to those around You. I want to have that same balance in my walk with You, hearing Your voice, doing and saying what I hear You say, doing what I see You do.

Please point out areas of my life where I am out of balance and taking on more responsibility than You designed for me. Forgive me for when and where I usurp Your place or think that I care more than You do. Show me what exercises or disciplines will develop the spiritual mobility and flexibility characteristic of a healthy strong spirit, improve my relationship with You, and bring You joy. I want to be balanced and grounded, that *"...workman who is not ashamed"* (2 Timothy 2:15). If I have harnessed myself to some responsibility that you did not give me, please forgive me for accepting it. Please reveal what the harness is so that I might repent and receive Your forgiveness. I want for there to be nothing holding me back in my walk with You, Jesus.

"And thine ears shall hear a word behind thee, saying, this is the way, walk ye in it, when ye turn to the right hand, and when ye turn to the left." (Isaiah 30:21).

Amen

The Importance of Intercession

I realized upon waking that I had had a night vision! At first you think it is a dream, but it is so vivid, so real that it feels like it actually happened. In it I saw a left leg, from the thigh to the toes, swollen, with streaks of blue, pink, and white. The ankle was the size of the knee and rolling over on itself. My first thought was, "Oh that has to hurt!" My next thought was, "Someone needs a massage to make the circulation start moving again!" And then I asked, "What is God saying?"

If that leg was a symbol for me personally, then I had a serious problem. I went to the Lord with questions from a spiritual angle:

What is blocking me spiritually?

What is blocking the flow of waste out of my body and spirit? Our bodies eliminate what has no more value, all the nutrients have been used up; we also eliminate the waste products of cells. If this flow of waste is blocked our bodies become ill quickly. The same process needs to happen spiritually—eliminate what God indicates no longer nourishes. Spiritual disciplines, church programs, or memberships in groups may have served us well for a time, but when the purpose the Lord had is finished, those activities no longer nurture and need to be re-evaluated. Some trimmed, and others eliminated. Waste can be an activity, an attitude, a habit, or even a discipline that was useful at one time, but is not anymore.

What am I retaining, or holding onto, that blocks the flow of the Holy Spirit?

How, and in what ways, am I spiritually inadequate in God's eyes?

What can I do to build a more adequate spiritual vessel? What character trait do I need to work on with God?

With whom should I talk about the spiritual bruising, inflammation, and infection in order to receive healing for my own spirit and soul?

After I addressed these questions, I asked the Lord to reveal whether these same questions, or others, should be applied to someone else (to whom?), or to our church. I used His answers to direct my intercession at that time for friends, family, my husband's work place and clients, as well as our church fellowship.

At that time, I was receiving a type of therapeutic massage that addresses a lymph edema problem secondary to MS. So rather than only entertain my own ideas about the dream, I asked my therapist what the picture meant to her. She sucked her breath in quickly and said, "In the natural that is a very serious condition. It is a picture of primary lymph edema, the result of vessels inadequately draining the leg of lymphatic fluid. The blue color indicates bruising from the swelling; the pink, inflammation; and the white, infection from lack of movement."

This dream was part of the fuel for writing *The Mystery of Spiritual Sensitivity*, a book that gives a biblical understanding of the concept of burden bearing. It also gives voice and vocabulary for how many highly sensitive people experience life. While meditating on this dream-vision, the Lord helped me understand that intercessors and burden-bearers are a vital part of the lymph system of the Body of Christ. Every Christian is to intercede for other Christians. Christ is seated at the right hand of God interceding and we are to do what he does. We are also outright commanded to pray for others many times. We are all called to bear one another's burdens (Galatians 6:2).

All is everyone. Additionally there are some who are called to a lifestyle of prayer and intersession, which is a bit more intense than what is expected of everyone else. As we all join Jesus in his work of intercession we keep His Body (the Church) cleansed, spiritually healthy, and functioning. But, if we are not interceding for members of The Body of Christ, contamination can build up and infect His Body—it can become sick, or ineffective. Christians in general, and intercessors in particular, are all part of the lymph system of the Church. Intercession is so essential to the health of the Church, it is a life and death matter.

Intercession cleanses The Body.

My therapist warned that if the leg were not treated, gangrene would soon set in and the limb could be lost. In the same way, we see churches closing and pastors leaving the ministry in alarming numbers. Looking at it with this new perspective made me see it as the Lord's

Body losing digits and limbs.

During the first year after the MS attack four different prophetic people, for whom I had great respect, came to me with a "word from the Lord." They each said that I was to write about my experiences with MS because [as] I was "going through this experience, what I would learn would also apply to the Church." What a puzzling word. If the things the Lord was teaching me would also apply to the Church, it would seem the Church has a serious problem, too. Some spiritual inadequacy that needed to be addressed sooner rather than later!

It seemed to me, a person with a leg so infected would not be able to function normally. Without intervention they would barely be able to take care of their personal needs, let alone overcome the infection. They would not have the energy to entertain thoughts of advancing in spiritual warfare, or setting captives free. Outside help would be needed! Now, I was beginning to see how intercessors also function as emergency workers, ICU workers, and the ones who are assigned to the ongoing health and well being of the Church (Body of Christ), both locally and worldwide. The Bible tells us the Body of Christ is to be the Church Victorious—something which indicates war. I can't see the Church Victorious shuffling into battle with a sword in one hand and a cane in the other. Or, taking a swing with that sword, becoming off balance, and going down in a heap!

That vision encouraged me to continue to intercede. I had to do what I could to prepare the way for The Coming King, and to encourage all those with the special calling of intercession to continue to intercede. The Father sees and takes note—our efforts are not in vain.

But, even as each of us prays for those in the patch God has assigned to us, we must also tend to our own spiritual health. We can refresh our own spirits with nature, art, and beauty.

We can balance spiritual activity with down-to-earth fun things, too. Fun things keep us from becoming overly serious and can flush any residue of the spiritual battlefield from our spirits. As I read Scripture, I see that Jesus rather enjoyed a good party! In fact, he was roundly criticized for keeping company with winebibbers and gluttons. *"Behold a man gluttonous, and a winebibber, a friend of publicans and sinners." (Matthew 11:19).*

But what about the times life becomes so difficult there is not the luxury of rest and refreshment? There will be those times. When we are not able to take care of ourselves, our Lord, Himself, provides what we need. Some of the greatest martyrs in history had only the beauty of Christ before them—they trained their eyes on Him, and they were fed richly. They were able to, with shining faces, say Father forgive them for they know not what they do. They were kept healthy spiritually by keeping their eyes on Jesus who is in heaven not on earth. Colossians 3:2 tells us to *"...set our minds on things above not on earthly things."*

I was beginning to discover that keeping a balance between spiritual and ordinary activities, as much as it was in my power to do so, keeps me from being infected spiritually, or inflamed with my own importance, thereby becoming an inadequate vessel. It also seems to result in living a more Christ-like life. The more of His character I allowed Him to build into my own, the more I would move toward becoming valuable. That one thing

I valued most of all, and felt like I had lost entirely.

 ## Ask the Holy Spirit

Using the same questions I asked myself, try going to the Holy Spirit for answers to your own situation:

- What is hindering my forward progress, blocking me spiritually?
- What is blocking the natural flow of eliminating waste--those things that no longer nurture or have spiritual value—a belief, an attitude, an activity, a habit?
- Why is it blocking me? What changes do I need to make?
- What am I retaining or holding onto that blocks the flow of the Holy Spirit?
- How, and in what ways, am I spiritually inadequate?
- What can I do to build a more adequate spiritual vessel?
- With whom should I talk about the spiritual bruising, inflammation, and infection I may have in order to receive healing?
- Ask Holy Spirit to reveal to you a new way to renew and cleanse your spirit so that you are able to do your part in the cleansing of His Body.

Prayer

Father, I praise you for your amazing love that makes

up for my inadequacies. I thank you for doing for me what I cannot do for myself. Things like salvation and restoration. Thank you for giving me the Holy Spirit as my coach, and teacher, as you train me in your ways, and build in reflexes that reflect the character and nature of your Son. I ask that you reveal to me areas that need more work, that need to be strengthened, where I need more growth; where the reflex is not dependable. Forgive me for hanging onto things that no longer nurture, for not moving on when you do. Enlarge my capacity for intercession so I can add to the strengthening of Your Body, so we can all move into the role of The Church Victorious.

"I praise you because *"I am fearfully and wonderfully made; your works are wonderful, I know that full well." (Psalm 139:14)*

Amen

Stained Glass Window

I was dreaming, again. This time, I found myself in a large abandoned sanctuary, which had been under renovation. Judging by the thick blanket of dust, the work had been abandoned for some time. The work of bringing glory to God had stopped. I knew, as one knows in dreams, that those who were supposed to be working had been called away to do laundry, wash dishes, mend clothes, do garden work, etc.

The cares of life had taken them captive. I could feel the frustration of those who had not wanted to leave the work. However, they were a people under authority, and orders were to be obeyed, like them or not. It must have seemed to some in authority that keeping body and soul together was a more pressing need than bringing glory to God, and therefore it received higher priority.

The sanctuary was dusty, dirty, nearly empty, and

obviously unused. A few items were stacked along one wall. A large table stood in the middle of the cavernous room. On it lay a partially completed stained glass window. The dust was so thick I didn't see it at first, but as I accidentally brushed some of the dust away, I realized what I was looking at. I quickly brushed more away to reveal a stunning portrait of Christ, nearly complete. I could tell that it was to be the centerpiece of the window, but the setting—the area surrounding Christ—was still unfinished. The pieces, all cut, lay scattered about the table in a jumble.

I looked up and saw the open window space in the wall, and then I glanced back at the stained glass work on the table. My finger traced over the lines of His face and I said to myself, "I can do this. This I can do. I know how to do this." On the surface I was speaking of putting together a stained glass piece because I had assisted a stained glass artist and knew the basics. An excitement began to bubble up within me as I sensed the Lord's pleasure in my desire to pick up the task of bringing glory to God.

Because of MS, I am not able to stand for the length of time needed to wash dishes or do laundry. Those ordinary jobs necessary for the keeping of body and soul together bring on crushing fatigue, but to sit at a table and put together this beautiful work of art? That I could do!

Again I knew with the knowing of dreams that for the foreseeable future the Lord was calling me aside for a deep inner work. On the natural plane I would be bringing glory to God through the medium of art, through the beauty of pottery, through the weaving of words, through the nurture that comes from the loving prayers stitched into a hand knit sweater. On a spiritual plane He was calling me aside for the work of organizing my life with Christ as the head, as the centerpiece. The result would be that people could see God clearly and be drawn to Him. I prayed that He would succeed!

Sitting in that dusty, quiet yet beautiful place, looking at those stained glass pieces, another knowing struck me. God was inviting me to release some of my housekeeping chores to able-bodied people. In that moment, my Uncle George's words came back to me. "I can't do what you do, but I can make money. I am very good at that. Let me do what I do best and you do what you do so well." I let my uncle help me through college then, and now in the sanctuary of my dream, the Lord was asking me to once again accept help from others.

It's not easy for me to let other people come into my home to do the simple tasks I've always done. Whenever I let someone help me, I battle with guilt feelings because I hear a lying voice in my head that says I am lazy or I am taking advantage of people's good will. My mind knows that is not true, but my emotions still sort of believe it. Now here was the Lord putting it all into perspective. It is not a matter of laziness or of taking advantage of others—it is a matter of doing what I can do best, and allowing others to do what they do best.

The next thing I became aware of was that I was alone in that huge sanctuary. As quickly as I realized it, I had an inner knowing that the task He was calling me to would be solitary. I could feel many people around me and I knew that I could be with them whenever I chose, but my work would be done alone, in the Lord's presence only. He would be the only one to know the true cost and the true value of that work. And that was okay. I enjoy The Lord's presence. Yes, He is King—the Lord God Almighty, Creator, my Savior, but He is also my friend. I like Him —and He is so good with color! I would enjoy the process of completing the likeness of His Son with Him.

I began to clean away the dust to arrange the pieces. As I did so, the Lord called my attention again to the space in the wall where the completed piece would rest. I gasped, for the completed piece was already installed and it was stunningly beautiful! Again I knew with the knowing of dreams that when people entered the sanctuary, the beauty of the window would take their breath away, and then after they came to themselves they would give glory to God. I had new energy and motivation to complete the portrait. I resumed arranging the pieces.

Then, just as the Lord could show me the completed window, even though the pieces lay on the table, He somehow revealed to me that I was the window and He was forming the likeness of His Son in me. As I put piece after piece where it would be permanently, I chuckled. *". . . till Christ be formed in you!" (Galatians 4:19)* So, Lord, that is what we are about! You are working on me, and with me, to form the nature and character of Christ in me! That is the work you are calling me to. So that when people are around me, they see You? Yes, that will be a solitary work and no one will know the cost to me, or the value to You." I can be part of a group, I can be among people, but the forming of Christ's image in me can only be done between God and me.

Shaking my head in amazement, I kept working to put the pieces in order. "Wow, God! You are something else! You said, ' . . . learn what pleases God.' (Ephesians 5:10) I know what pleases You. When Jesus was baptized and began His work of reconciliation, as He came up out of the water, You said, *'This is my Son, in whom I am well pleased.' (Matthew 3:17)* As I arrange my life in such a way that it reveals Jesus nature and character, as I pour myself out in the ministry of reconciliation, that pleases You, my Father!"

There is a way in which Christ's nature will be formed in me. The work will be done to me, and it is not something I do by my own effort. But there is also an aspect in which I do have a very active part. My part is to hold myself in a place where God can work on me. I can be still, like the window on the table, and not flee or resist, or bombard Him with a running critique or commentary. I can work spiritual disciplines into my life. I can submit to His direction in choosing friends and activities. I can choose to be obedient to His direction in regard to balance in all areas of life.

These pieces of my life I can choose to organize under His direction rather than choosing my own design. The Holy Spirit will provide the stuff that binds the pieces together in the design that results in abundance of glory to God, and the most joy and fulfillment for me!

Once again, He called my attention to the window space in the sanctuary. This time I saw The Good Shepherd with arms extended in invitation. I thought, "But that is a different piece than the one I am working on!" I must have immediately gone to worry that He was asking me to take on a second window before I finished the first because He calmed my fear. He communicated that this was a picture to clarify what He was saying in the first window. He caused me to know that a life in which Christ has been formed will be an invitation, and people will be drawn to Him.

As I studied The Good Shepherd my attention was drawn to the colors of the stained glass. They were vivid; they danced with life. How can colored glass take on life? Somewhere in my reading over the years I think I read that lead was used to create the vibrant colors, but that it is used no longer since discovering that lead is poisonous. This is the reason we cannot find colored glass with the vibrancy of color we see in the very old cathedrals of Europe. I thought, yes, you don't often see that kind of color, that kind of vibrant life—the kind that attracts people to the Good Shepherd. It made me sad. I could not say if it was my sadness or the Father's. Probably both. But again, I knew that as I worked with beauty, the beauty would draw people to the Good Shepherd who is full of life and gives life. How ironic that one who battles constantly with balance issues and fatigue would call others to liveliness!

Over and over again these pictures and thoughts tumbled though my mind, drawing me again and again into the Father's presence to ponder these things. Finally, after three weeks, I saw something I had not seen before! From time to time someone asks why I think God has not healed me of MS. I haven't been sure, but I've steadfastly held that God is good and that I want to learn everything He can possibly teach me through it.

The enemy conspired to bring together the right (or wrong, depending on how you look at it) mix of people and circumstances to throw my body chemistry off balance and lower my immune system. At the opportune time he launched a spiritual attack. In a physically weakened state I could not repel an attack on both fronts.

The enemy meant to take me out permanently, but the result was only to remove me from the busy activities of life—it made me more like Mary and less like Martha.

And, as I sit at Christ's feet and His likeness is formed in me, others will come to the Good Shepherd, be reconciled to Him, and all glory will go to God. Christ being formed in me transforms my pain into a pane through which the Son shines, causing the individual pieces to dance with vibrant life and spill glory throughout the sanctuary.

My stance of wanting to learn everything God can teach me through this journey has been like the pole for a vaulter. I set my will to learn from God like the vaulter sets his pole, and that stance vaulted me into the process of Christ being formed in me. I have landed much further ahead than I would have, had the enemy left me alone. The very force of the death-thrust Satan hurled at me was what God used to accelerate the formation of Christ in me. Is that redemptive suffering? It is certainly suffering redeemed.

When I first discovered the window in pieces on the table, Christ, as the centerpiece, was complete. Everything around Him waited to be put in place. This was a picture to me of how my loving Father, knowing how I am made, knew exactly the lines along which I would break and here was His promise to me of making something beautiful of my shattered life. His design, as the jumbled pieces of my life come together around Christ, will result in the optimum refraction of His light and glory. How comforting to know that the Lord is overseeing this glorious work of art!

God's goal all along has been the development of value

in my life in preparation for my ultimate destiny! Like a lover, He has been jealous to have my time and attention, knowing that we become like those with whom we associate. He knew that one day I would agree with the course that He chose, but at the time I had neither the maturity nor perspective to comprehend the ultimate goal. He was willing to put up with my upset, emotional outbursts, accusations, and occasional bouts of despondency because of the joy we would be able to share! I am so grateful He did not give up on me! We serve a very big and loving God.

 ## Ask the Holy Spirit

God calls you to do that which is appropriate for you. Sometimes family and society agree with you on what's appropriate. Sometimes not. The "sometimes nots" are what twist you into knots and push you into duty even if it is not appropriate for you! Take some time to ask God for discernment in regard to what he is calling you to do.

> ➤ Ask Him if there are areas of your life where you are carrying an inappropriate load. Ask Him what changes you need to make to correct this, and ask Him to show you the proper time to make the changes.
> ➤ We are works of art in the hands of a gentle, tender artist who does fabulous, meticulous work—He wastes nothing. He will move all the pieces of your life into place in a way that will reflect and refract His glory. If you are willing to submit to His hand in your life you will come into joy and

fulfillment! Ask Him to point out areas where you are unwilling to submit.
- Ask Him what needs to change so that you can submit.
- How does this sanctuary (unused, dusty, etc.) reflect the condition of your spirit?
- During the times when you cannot see the big picture ask to see with His eyes. Ask Him what is hindering you from seeing with the eyes of heaven.
- Ask if there are scales on your eyes and if they can be removed.
- Is there something that needs attention before the scales can be removed?
- If you still cannot see, it is a time to hold very still in His hands while He sets a fragile piece into place—trust His process! He is making your life a work of such beauty it will take your breath away. Ask for more grace to hold still!

Prayer

Father I thank you for the privilege of being part of refracting the glory and beauty of Your Son. I bless Your plans for You have a much bigger, more beautiful picture of my life than I, and I have confidence that You will lovingly assemble my shattered bits to achieve the optimum glory of Your Son. As much as I am able, I willingly submit to Your process and ask that You point out to me the areas where I can cooperate and what I can do to enhance what You are doing.

Forgive me for the times I slip into duty and take on

things that are inappropriate for me. Please remove any scales from my eyes so that I can join You in seeing Your process and my life with the eyes of heaven. Show me where I am resisting Your process.

My heart is to reflect Your love, goodness and beauty; to do my bit to *"provide for those who grieve in Zion— to bestow on them a crown of beauty instead of ashes, the oil of joy instead of mourning, and a garment of praise instead of a spirit of despair. They will be called oaks of righteousness, a planting of the Lord for the display of his splendor." (Isaiah 61:3)*

Amen

Stay The Course

I spend far more time with my feet elevated than I'd like. MS fatigue can be debilitating. It kills my drive. One day, while sitting quietly in my recliner knitting, I became aware of another reality. It was spooky to feel the knitting needles in my hands but see another reality. It was like having a dream with my eyes open! I saw a planet from the perspective of a distant orbit, like a scene from *Star Trek* where the *Enterprise* hangs motionless in space when approaching a huge sphere. I saw a net, made of vines, cast over the planet as if it were to be pulled.

I asked the Lord if the planet were earth and was given, "When I created earth I put it in a safe place." He didn't exactly answer my question, but I thanked the Lord for that assurance, knowing that any place other than where God put the earth would not be safe. I knew, as one knows things without being expressly told, that the net was an evil thing pulling the world off course. I asked Him how to pray about this scene and heard, "Stay the course." I prayed as God instructed. That He would "stay the course" of earth—its spiritual, historical, and physical course. I then saw the planet with a rod sticking through the poles to hold it in place and the net was gone.

Then, a huge door in the planet opened up. I observed the door opening and was, at the same time, on the planet as part of a group of people who were opening the door. (It was a very strange feeling to have two perspectives at the same time and also be aware of my physical surroundings!) I knew that I was to invite the Lord in. *"Thy Kingdom come, Thy will be done on earth as it is in Heaven" (Matthew 6:10).* I imagine that I felt as Noah must have felt opening the door of the ark! There was a sense of great excitement on both the physical and the spiritual levels. I knew that we would be inviting the Lord to take the driver's seat in our lives, individually, nationally, and globally—we were inviting Him into our corporate lives. He could put on the brakes or make whatever course corrections were needed. We were inviting Him to be the driving force in our lives.

Physically speaking, if Satan were to pull the planet even the barest bit out of its prescribed orbit the gravitational pull on the earth would cause great upheaval in the oceans and the atmosphere.

One wonders about the weather these days . . .

Spiritually speaking, the net is used in the occult and represents the strongholds all over the world. The net was woven together—strongholds interlocking and working in concert with each other to enmesh and ensnare people —to pull them off balance and off course. The enemy would like to use this network of strongholds to pull people, societies—even history and the future—off course and into destruction. History reveals the enemy's plan of trying to preempt what God is doing—to make something happen prematurely. He tried to kill Moses before his time, he tried to kill David before his time, and he tried to kill Jesus before His time.

God seems to need access to our engines—our core—so He can do the course corrections needed to put us back on track, and bring our life into balance. He, alone, has the wisdom, power, and ability to make corrections in a safe way. If we try to make the corrections by ourselves, we risk overcorrecting and flying out of the safe orbit the Lord ordained for each one of us.

Since I told the Lord that I wanted to learn everything I could possibly learn from this disease, my default question during recovery became: What is the spiritual significance? I seemed to focus more on why the symptom was present in my life rather than solely concentrating on how to rid myself of it. My belief was that all of life's circumstances are Father filtered. If there is a physical dysfunction it was probably the physical manifestation of some spiritual reality—if the spiritual reality is the cause (or part of the cause) and if that is addressed, the symptom should disappear. The question of why it was present in my life became, in a sense, a search for a cure; but from a spiritual plane rather than the physical plane alone. I would let the research scientists work on the physical plane while I worked on the spiritual plane.

Lack of visual clarity was among the difficulties I had to contend with as a consequence of MS. I simply do not see clearly. I miss details. For example, I don't see dust, or spills on the floor; buttons, pins and paper clips easily escape me. I discover I have dropped ice when I step in the puddle! When my slipper sticks to the floor I know I spilled something and the floor needs attention. That is not an excuse to delay cleaning the kitchen—I simply don't see these kinds of details unless I am very close or it is really bad!

I pondered with The Almighty the spiritual significance of not seeing clearly. The results of that pondering surprised me. My sense was that my belief in my insignificance, my lack of importance to God and my lack of value to others, so clouded my vision I could not see Him clearly, nor the vision of what He wanted to show me. My own beliefs limited what He could do for me, through me, and in me.

I gulped, but He was not finished.

He added that I fear failure, and the fear of failure and loss holds me back. If I were to see what He has planned and wants to do together with me, and if I were to step out into that plan and begin to work it out, fear of failure would grip me and hold me back—but it does not have to be that way! The significance to me was to understand that the actual physical impairment is a metaphor to help me face and deal with my issue of feeling insignificant and unimportant, of little value to self, God or others. My belief was a slap in the face to a God who gave His own son for me! Long pause needed here to let this sink in!

God is so gracious! At a moment when I could have begun to crumple from the weighty conviction of truth, He gently reminded me that I have worked hard and faithfully for many years. He notices, He remembers and cares! I sensed Him invite me to see where He was leading, fully knowing that emotionally I would crumple and not want to look for fear that His plan is too wonderful. And I truly would enjoy it so much! He knew that when I followed Him and began to succeed, the fear would arise ... that the wonderful plan would then be taken away. Both success and failure would result in loss.

He knows that there is a big part of me that does not want to go through the pain of loss, again. That fear of success and or failure, and subsequent loss, keeps me from looking. It keeps my faith from rising up. It also prevents Him from sending the provision to do what He is calling me to do! Which saddens Him greatly.

My eyes do not change focus quickly anymore, either. When I focus, what I am looking at must be in the center of my visual area. Objects and people in my peripheral vision flip, slide, or dance all over. The MS caused me to have a downbeat nystagmus which means the image slides downward and then my eye muscles jerk back to center, only to slide away and be jerked back again. If I look at my feet when I walk the flipping becomes more rapid. Add a downward incline and the ground begins to swim. I am never sure of where to place my foot!

Looking to the side in a moving car is even worse. The passing view is a blur and I am unable to distinguish one object from another. You can see why I gave up driving. I realized that I did not know which of those three cars to avoid! The more I concentrate, as in driving, the quicker muscles fatigue which makes the problem worse! The same thing happens when I read. The effort of holding the line of print still fatigues the muscles and soon I have to rest my eyes. I am no longer a speed reader and the larger the font the better! The length of time I can focus is much less, so it appears that my attention span has decreased when it is a matter of muscle fatigue. And, the sliding of the focus causes me to sometimes focus on the wrong thing.

I was on the third floor of a beautiful old lodge, standing on a stair when the original attack happened. Suddenly everything went flat; the stair disappeared. I held fast to the handrail and sat down. Like a child learning to navigate stairs, I bounced down to the floor below. Using the wall as my guide, I managed to navigate the hallway to my room. The difficulty seeing depth continues today. When I walk on sidewalks I am careful to stop, find the edge of the curb with my toe, and then step down. I cannot see the depth difference between curb and street. I check for it with my toe only because my mind knows it is probably there. There have been some times where I did not see, did not check, and walked as though there was no curb. The jolt was hard. Being unable to discern in depth is a serious spiritual problem because of the eternal consequences of missteps.

I took all these issues to meditation with the Lord and learned a great deal. I must come to the place where I admit that on my own I cannot accomplish and sustain anything. Whatever I accomplish is by His grace. He is the author and the perfecter (or finisher) of my faith (Hebrews 12:2). How wonderful to know that God does not abandon work He begins! I must focus on Him—at all times, in every season! I must learn to hear and recognize His voice directing me where to place my foot and to verify my perceptions!

Spiritually speaking, I need to be able to discern so that I do not stumble and fall. A stumbling block is just that—a stumbling block—because I do not perceive it to be what it is! I need to be able to distinguish one object from another; especially, I need to be able to distinguish between the spiritual and the natural so that I can recognize the enemy and his snares. I also need to discern so that I am not afraid—the tears that come from grief, loss, bitterness, or fear can cause many objects to morph together and look like huge scary monsters or take the "bumps out of the road" when in reality, the bumps remain. Jesus wants to dry my tears and clear my vision so that my steps can be confident and sure.

Ask the Holy Spirit

First, ask Him the list of questions that follow and listen for the thoughts that come to you and write them down. Notice the emotions that arise, any pictures or visions He gives you . . . and write them down. Think deeply on what He tells you, and then pray about each aspect that He reveals to you. His aim is that we become holy. We become holy when we make the decision to change what He shows us needs to change, and then do the hard work to change. He is right there, in the hard place, with all the grace we need; helping us make the godly choice!

- ➢ Lord, in what way am I not seeing you clearly?
- ➢ In what way is my vision limited when You would want to change or enlarge it?
- ➢ What do I need to hold on to in order to remain balanced and grounded?
- ➢ Am I unable to focus? Or, am I focusing on the wrong thing?

- ➢ Why is my attention span so short—why can I not tolerate sustained effort?
- ➢ Ask Him to reveal the passions He deposited in you.
- ➢ Ask Him to show you how the enemy gained access to your passions, either to misdirect them or to push you to go beyond what God is asking of you.
- ➢ Ask Him to reveal changes you can make to prevent this access.
- ➢ Ask for His strategy and timing to begin making these changes.

Prayer

Thank you, Father, for revealing danger while there is still time to call on You. Help us to stay the course You have called us to, as individuals, as families, as churches, as the Body of Christ at large, as a society, and as a nation. We pray that the enemy not be allowed to ensnare peoples and nations, to pull them into harm's way and into destruction. That you will defeat the strongholds in our lives, family, church, society, and nation. Jesus, we invite You into our world, and our universe, to do what needs to be done to stay the course of our lives, our families, and society.

" . . . *with your strong arm you scattered your enemies.*" *(Psalm 89:10b)*

Amen

No Fears

I awoke realizing I had been given another dream from the Lord! In my dream, I was part of a group on some kind of hike, or quest. Point to note: I was part of a group —this rarely happens. Since MS, two or three is enough of a group for me, but this was maybe a dozen! First, I saw three wall panels slide to the side, and suddenly I was in a different environment.

The area was filled with dense vegetation. It felt like Central America but without any oppressive humidity and heat. As the group progressed, we came into a cleared area. However, our way was completely blocked by some kind of monolithic construction that had a spiritual force coming from it. I would not approach the thing. I backed away, saying, "Oh, God, this is not You—no way. I have seen enough of You to know; this is not You!" As I meditated, asking God, I got the sense that this was an idol. I questioned, was it a personal idol, regional, national, or something else?

As I meditated on the dream more and talked with Father, I came to believe that it was a territorial spirit. Its purpose was to block the believer from moving forward into intimacy with God. As new Christians, it is natural for us to press into Jesus, and strive to mature. But after some time and maturity, we come to a place where the Lord can reveal Himself and begin to give us spiritual experiences. This idol thing seemed to have set itself up at that very juncture, and tried to take credit for the "spiritual" experiences, frightening believers, so that they would stop short of what God had for them. In the dream I saw that on the other side of the idol was a portal —I don't know if it is a place of revelation or a place for actually going somewhere—like maybe a quick peek into heaven!

The idol that had been set up in front of it looked like some kind of monolithic Mayan god, which—to me— indicated it had been enthroned in that area for a very long time. By that particular area I mean whenever (or wherever) a believer comes into a place where they can finally see. Somehow I knew that corporate intercession for Central America would not unseat this thing! All of us would have to deal with it, individually, in order to continue on this path.

I asked if I could please step into an angel, and maybe be hidden to go past the thing.

I was told, "No. You were given this dream for a reason."

Yikes! God wants me to actually do something about it! My reaction was to back away. In a hushed tone I said, "God, this is a territorial spirit! These are big dudes! You don't just mess with these guys!"

God cleared His throat.

I said, "Oh, yeah. You are bigger and more powerful

than any territorial spirit!"

Then He reminded me that I was with a group. I was not being asked to take it on alone.

Whew!

Later, I shared my dream with the only group I am a part of that I have confidence in regarding spiritual things of this magnitude. I asked them to share it with those who test spirits, and interpret dreams. I didn't want to start to pray until the troops were gathered. In the meantime, I continued to meditate (think about) the dream, as well.

My conclusion from that meditation is this: each believer before going into intercession must face off with his/her fear. Each of us has fear of something. Fear of God (in a negative way) goes all the way back to the Garden of Eden. Fear of the unknown, of change, of what God will do with me, or to me; fear of what will happen to me if I throw caution to the wind and follow Him. Fear of man is a big deal, too, as well as the loss of friends, family, or finances. Thinking about these things, I felt sure if any of us begins to intercede for the dethronement of this—or any entity—without first tending to these personal fears, it will push back and kick off one or more of those very same fears. Then we will be tempted to stop short of that more personal walk with God. Either that, or we will be captured in some way, and led astray.

I had never been involved in intercession of this magnitude, so I appreciated having others who were more knowledgeable and experienced than I, to head up the intercession. I didn't want to be hurt, nor did I want to invite someone into intercession and have them become crème de la Christian!

Meanwhile, I began to inspect this idol thing in the

spirit. That's when I saw what looked like a school building behind the thing—an institution! Directly in front of the school building was the idol. Closer inspection revealed that the idol was actually the front of the building. What did that mean? My sense was that some fears are so socially acceptable that we actually teach them to others.

We have institutionalized our fears!

And in Matthew 5:17-19 Jesus said, *"Do not think that I have come to abolish the law or the prophets. I have come not to abolish them, but to fulfill them. Truly I say to you, until heaven and earth pass away, not an iota, not a dot will pass from the law until all is accomplished. Therefore, whoever relaxes one of the least of these commandments and teaches others to do the same will be called least in the kingdom of heaven, but whoever does them and teaches them will be called great in the kingdom of heaven."*

Selah (the Hebrew word which means "Think about that.")

My God, I do not want to have a wrong fear of you and then compound that sin by institutionalizing it and teaching it to others! That would be truly leading someone astray.

I heard from the Lord that we should attack its foundation, not a frontal assault, but pick away at its foundation. By taking away chunks of its foundation it would become unbalanced and the very weight of the thing would make it fall! Then He showed me that after repenting of my fears, I was to dance in worship in front of this thing!

That made my stomach twist until He calmed me with

the assurance that the vibrations of the dance would be what caused the idol to begin to tip, and then its weight would take it down. He was calling me to dance into war, as the Children of Israel did in ancient times. Amazing! It seemed all I had to do was repent of fear, and dance before the Lord in the clearing. I was dancing before the LORD, NOT the idol! He would be responsible for the frontal confrontation of the spirit behind the idol. Repentance and dancing seemed doable, confrontation did not! NOTE: *"God dwells in the praises of his people." (Psalm 22:3)* As His Body, we are to go forth for him, as he directs. He accomplishes His work (or finishes it) through us.

Then I heard the echo of an earlier word: "There are many ways to war." Picking the stones out of a foundation (stones, as in stumbling blocks) may not seem like spiritual warfare. Facing our own spiritual fears may not seem like warfare. But anything that will topple an entrenched idol is most definitely warfare! Facing our fears is worth the freedom that comes from that decision all by itself. Even if we scrape our knuckles, become grubby, and all hot and sweaty in the process.

As I approached dealing with my fears, I realized I didn't really know how to do that. If all fear is a lack of trust, how do you repent of lack of trust? How do I make a 180-degree turn and go the other way to walk in faith, instead, when I have this lack of trust that I am carrying around? That's when I become aware that my mind does not want the fear. And my spirit's resolve, determination, and desire, is to trust God totally. It is in my soul where the fear lies. That fear creeps out like a vine and trips up my will, hobbles my spirit. So impeded, I inadvertently step on a puffball, that emits a smokescreen to confuse the issues, distract attention, and darken my mind. Fear is insidious!

One might ask, "What fears?"

They are multitude: Fear of success and fear of failure—what a double bind! Fear of lack—lack of provision, or finances. Lack of place, such as home and church fellowship. Lack of opportunity, especially economic opportunity, and ministry. Fear of falling short, and fear of inadequacy physically, spiritually, and emotionally. Fear of not being able to endure (that fatigue will take me out of play). Fear of the unknown—both in this world and in spiritual realms. Fear of missing my moment, or missing what God is doing. Those fears seem to cover all of life, in this world as well as the spiritual realm. Good grief—that's a pretty pervasive list!

I had never seen myself as fearful or fear-driven—the Lord had to show me, in that dream, just how hidden those fears had become. The Lord explained to me that the first wall panel I had seen slide to the side when my dream began, represented the veil between the spiritual and the natural. The second represented the layers of fears cloaking (or hiding) the idol. And the third represented the deceptions that covered my own personal fears.

Going back to the dream, itself, our group had stepped into a clearing—a place where we could see. As we continued to move forward, the Lord caused a clearing of our vision, so we could see plainly what was blocking our path into what He had prepared for us.

When facing fear, I have found it comforting to remember what I know and have personally experienced. For me it is this: The Lord has always made things work out. He made a way where there seemed to be no way. He provided food for the table, a roof over my head, and a job for me to do. He has always given direction and comfort when I was hurting. He never called me to do anything I was not able to accomplish. He has given me creativity, ingenuity, and insight. He has taken me places, and shown me things in the spirit. He always protected me. Which—in my estimation—gives Him a pretty good record.

So, if I am to proceed along the path God has put me on, I must pass that idol of fear. I must dethrone the fear from my heart and enthrone Jesus, instead! He must reign supreme over my spirit, soul, and body. I can uproot and overturn that huge idol only by conquering the fears which form the foundation upon which it sits!

As I thought and prayed about all of this, I felt a coating flowing down from my head, over my shoulders and down my front. Anointing? His blood as a protection? Or both?

 ## Ask the Holy Spirit

> ➤ At this point, I encourage you to ask Father God to protect and anoint you as you take on the task of dethroning your own fears. Start with the little ones; many small fears removed make a big hole in the foundation upon which that spirit enthrones itself to purposefully hinder your spiritual maturity and intimacy with God. It is even okay to ask for a dream to help expose them to you so you know what you are dealing with. But when you "do your dance of praise," whether it be physically dancing or spiritually dancing (some

of us have balance issues or health issues that make it necessary to "arm dance" from our recliners or beds); remember that you dance before the Lord. Look always to Him; keep your eyes on Him, for He is always faithful to protect and deliver. And He will make a way as you worship. Praise is a powerful weapon.

In my mind's eye I can see the movie *Land Before Time*. There was one scene in which the dinosaurs found a way through the rubble of the earthquake and discovered the Lost World—the world that was made for them. In the same way, many of us "old dinosaurs" have been prevented from being, doing, and living in the realm God created for us—from our destiny. I believe dance and praise are important. Because the Lord uses the vibrations set off by them [in the spiritual realm] to unbalance the huge, ancient idols: those old fears that have held us all back for so long.

➢ And finally, ask the Lord for a dream of your own; ask Him for a strategy that will work best against the fears that have enthroned themselves in your life. He is faithful and will do it. He will deliver and protect.
➢ Ask the Lord to touch your spiritual eyes so that you can see as He sees.
➢ Ask the Lord how He views these hard experiences of your life.
➢ Ask in what way have you misinterpreted the hard experiences of your life.
➢ Ask the Lord to show you what your fears are—

your stumbling blocks, your idols.
- ➢ Ask Him for His strategy for you to make war and have victory over them.
- ➢ Ask for the Lord's timing for implementing His strategy.

Prayer

Holy Spirit, empower me; enlarge my capacity to trust You, Father. Following the lead of Your Holy Spirit, I ask You to find each and every fear I am aware of, and that You reveal those of which I am unaware. Jesus, Your word says, *"...by Your stripes we are healed." (Isaiah 53:5)* Apply Your life blood with power to heal and bring life to the wound and/or disappointments that led to the fear, as well as all the hurts that piled up and confirmed it. Help me understand what I need to know so that I am not tripped up, pushed back into those fears, and taken captive all over, again.

May I be single-minded and have an undivided heart. Please, Lord, shield my emotions, and defend me against the pressure and accusation of the rude Philistines employed by that territorial spirit. I ask that You reign over this territory in my life, instead. I declare that You alone are Lord. I pray that You will take up my cause and confront the idol. Holy Spirit, teach me to trust and not fear!

I praise You Jesus, for You have overcome. All power has been given to You, Lord Jesus. I praise and dance before You in the presence of my enemies. In the clearing, in the place where I have new vision and can finally see, I praise Your name!

"Lord, You are my shepherd, I lack nothing. You make me lie down in green pastures, and lead me beside quiet waters. You refresh my soul. You guide me along the right paths for Your name's sake. Even though I walk through the darkest valley, I will fear no evil, for you are with me; Your rod and your staff, they comfort me. You prepare a table before me in the presence of my enemies. You anoint my head with oil; my cup overflows. Surely your goodness and love will follow me all the days of my life, and I will dwell in the house of the Lord forever." (Psalm 23).

Amen.

Part Three
HIS VOICE

The Joy of The Lord

My Christian friend, meaning to encourage me, slaps me on the shoulder and assures me that "the joy of the Lord is your strength!" I nod in agreement and give a cheesy smile. It has become another Christian platitude and does not carry much meaning for me, let alone strength. Strength and energy are what I need, not buzz words and phrases! What is the joy of the Lord anyway, and how in the world does it strengthen you?

Over the years I have come face to face with what I called a lack of motivation. I could see what I needed to do, but I could not move my body to do it. I delved into negative self-talk and labeled the lack of movement as lack of motivation. Days turned into months and years with no change. I feared that I had lost my vision. I could no longer picture myself serving or ministering—how could I help others when I needed help myself! Was sitting on God's shelf to be my new destiny? I know that just being God's friend is a worthy thing. But somehow being only a pretty pot on God's shelf didn't fit me—it didn't feel quite right. I couldn't seem to say, "For this I was born!"

Maybe I needed a new "post MS vision." I asked the Lord, but I received nothing new. All I could do was write the things He showed me from time to time; visit with folks, and do that intercessory prayer thing. As life went on, that didn't seem like much of a contribution. Especially when I push myself to do and go, and be present, I experience an exhaustion that leaves me feeling cored out. It is a physical pain.

I explain to people that I have to be quiet and relatively inactive for two or three days and let the energy return. It is like a slow spring; use all the water in the pool and you will have to wait for more to collect. Leave the spring undisturbed and the water will seep in and fill the pool again—but stay out of it until it is full! For me this means, "My bucket is empty. Go away and leave me alone until my energy returns. Don't bang around trying to get something from me when I've nothing to give. The most you'll get is a snarl!"

That kind of exhaustion means that not only have I used all of my own resources, I have also exhausted the grace God gave me for the day. Remember, He says, *"His Mercies (compassions) are new "every morning." (Lam. 3:22, 23)* If I use all of today's grace by 10:30 a.m., I am going to have to be very careful with my reactions to people. I will have to work hard to make sure my responses are grace-full!

Scripture says in Nehemiah 8:10 that *"the joy of the Lord is your strength!"* But when we say, "the joy of the Lord," do we mean a joy that belongs to the Lord? Did it originate with Him, or is this joy my own emotional response to being in the presence of the Lord? The Hebrew Bible makes it clear that the joy does belong to the Lord. He is a fountain of joy that is inside me, once I ask Him to be my Savior. I have access to joy because it is resident within me. All I have to do is run to it. He is my fortress, a high tower (Psalm 18:2). Then I understood what Jesus was talking about when He prayed for His disciples that they would be able to abide in Him that their joy may be complete (mature, fully developed) (John 15:11).

Choices again. I can choose to remain in my blue funk, or turn from it to face The Joy of My Life. The blue funk will suck every last ounce of energy if I do not stop it. Hopefully, I can stop it before that happens, but if it has a strong hold on me, even in those moments when I feel the last bits of energy slipping from me, I can choose to use that little bit of remaining energy to focus on Jesus. When I focus on Him, and turn away from concentrating on negative circumstances, I feel my spirits rise, and my energy returns.

Joy is the source of my energy! When He said, *"Apart from Me you can do nothing." (John 15:5b),* He was not joking. He was not being poetic. He was stating a fact. He is the source of joy; joy produces energy—no joy, no energy. Literally, apart from Him I do not have energy to do anything!

Another scripture leaped to life. *"Whoever believes in me, as Scripture has said, rivers of living water will flow from within them."(John 7:38a)* Living water. Water that is living is moving; moving water produces energy. Just stand at the base of Niagara Falls and feel the power of the moving water! Water that does not move is stagnant; it stinks, and it does not sustain much life. What life it does sustain is not generally healthy.

As I was trying to incorporate this internal explosion, the Lord posed another scripture. *"Thy kingdom come, Thy will be done on earth as it is in heaven..." Matt. 6:10* Simultaneously, I saw what I can only describe as a zone—a place on my inner landscape—that was illuminated. I knew, without words, that this was Jesus—Christ in me; the hope of glory—my safety zone. (Col. 1:27) He is the place where I can come to find living water, peace, direction, safety; everything I needed—this was Joy's Place. I knew that I needed to learn how to make this my home as well.

Jesus—this place of joy—is my "high tower, my refuge, my fortress." I have to learn how to live in joy and approach life from the place of joy in a way I had, up to that point, not known. It is there for me; it has been all along. Now that I am aware of it, I need to learn what causes me to lose my way. What dulls—or lulls—my senses so I cannot perceive joy. I need to find out, so I can avoid those things at all costs.

Again, He communicated without words that my presence there in the Joy Zone increases God's "overflowing gaiety." The zone will become larger and larger as I spend more time there, until my entire inner landscape becomes saturated with joy that has overflowed from God, who is happy that I choose to abide where He lives. This is not to turn inward away from life, but to do life from the place of joy—to do life from within the zone rather than just near the zone.

When I stopped bouncing off the walls with all that joy, I had a very serious question. How can I be a believer, have Jesus resident in my life, He who is the origin of joy, and not be able to experience enough joy to be able to function, at least to a minimal level? His response to the question was quick. I had no sooner asked than the following verse came to mind:

"But he said to me, 'My grace is sufficient for you, for my power is made perfect in weakness.' Therefore, I will boast all the more gladly about my weaknesses, so that Christ's power may rest on me." (2 Corinthians 12:9).

Well, according to that Scripture, I am in some way not accessing or availing myself of resources that I already have. I certainly am not boasting about or glorying in my infirmity! How can I be grateful to God for my infirmities? What needs to be different?

I thought He should flood my body with strength, first, then my life would demonstrate the power of God, and I could go about serving others. That would produce joy. However, I began to see how that would actually enable my flawed humanity. The belief that I must earn love and belonging is not the truth, yet that was my foundation.

A step further and I could see that if the Lord gave me strength and power, first, I would have enough energy to continue to perform and do good works. I might think, and feel, that I was demonstrating the power of God, but I would be doing it from a foundational belief that love and belonging must be earned. Yes, some good would happen. But I would also reproduce that same foundation in others, perpetuating the erroneous belief that love and belonging go only to those who serve Him.

I could see then that He wanted to give me a new foundation: one built on truth. I was first conceived in His mind—He loved me then and I belonged to Him then. Only later was I conceived in my mother's womb Jeremiah 1:5. He gave me love and belonging from the moment He conceived me in His mind. Nothing I could do will ever make Him love me more—or less.

I saw that—up until then—I had been living close to the outer edge of that illuminated spot on my inner landscape, the spot in me where His Joy resides. I have lived near His Joy and often felt the mist of that fountain. I knew there was more but my focus had been turned away from Joy toward the people and circumstances of my life, instead.

Suddenly I could see how I needed to turn around. To face the Joy, and then look at life through the filter (or lens) of His Joy. That would prime the pump of joy within me, causing His Joy to bubble up, overflow, and totally saturate my inner landscape. Fully saturated, joy would overflow out of me into every place I went. Then when I collided with life—or it with me—I will splash joy rather than spew anger, or leak irritation. Because when I am weak, I cannot perform. Instead, I must receive— both from the Lord, and from others. I needed to learn how to exercise the grace that He gave me each day to receive from Him. To receive it in joy, and joy would abound.

Incredible! I realized I had just had a very specific conversation with the Lord, without a physical word being spoken. And yet, I knew. Then—as if that was not enough—He communicated to me that this place of joy is where Heaven touches down. I have repeated The Lord's Prayer countless times. *"Thy kingdom come, Thy will be done on earth as it is in heaven..." (Matthew 6:10)* but I never gave it much thought. My feeling was that Jesus will come when He gets here! I never gave much thought to whether or not I could hasten that coming. Now if I understood Him correctly, He was saying:

"Your coming to the Fountain of Life, the place in your inner being where I choose to dwell, will hasten My coming, for that place of joy is the spot where Heaven and earth meet. If you choose to live near My Joy rather than in My Joy you choose to live without access to your power source. You will live on "battery power." But your continual presence with Me enlarges the connection between Heaven and earth. The greater the connection, the more of My kingdom has come! It, and all its resources, is at hand. Right now. This is how you can hasten My will to be done in the earth—to purposefully, intentionally pursue joy. Joy energizes you—it is the source of your strength—it literally causes your physical brain to activate the energy to do life."

Wow, frontwards and backwards! Wow! We really are fearfully and wonderfully made! Having joy, we are able to catch a vision that will direct and carry the energy that joy activates in us. God is our one and only true source of joy (strength and energy). Without Him, we can do nothing.

 ## Ask the Holy Spirit

- When you lack motivation repent of turning away, or wandering away from your energy source.
- Receive His forgiveness and ask Him to bring you back to your source of joy.
- Ask Him to show you how and where you went off

track.
- Ask Him to show you why you went off track.
- Ask Him what changes you need to make to stay on the path He set you on.
- Ask Him to show you how He is using the hard places in your life to build the character and nature of Jesus into you.
- Ask for Him to teach you His ways so that you are not easily led off course.
- God first conceived you in His mind. You were conceived in your mother's womb later. Nothing you can ever do or not do will make Him love you more or less. He loved you then and He loves you still. Record your mental, emotional, and spiritual reactions.

Prayer

Thank you God that You had me in Your mind long before I was conceived in my mother's womb. Nothing I can ever do or not do will make You love me more or less. You loved me then and You love me still. I repent and ask Your forgiveness for turning away, or wandering away from you, my energy source. I receive Your forgiveness and ask You to bring me back to You and restore my joy.

Father show me how and why I went off track—was I deceived, driven off, or was I tempted? Please teach me Your ways so that I can build them into my life and stay on the path You set for me. Help me understand how You are using the hard places in my life to build the character and nature of Jesus into me so that I will not be tempted to complain or accuse You and I will not easily be led astray.

And on those days when my strength fails me draw me close to You that I might be renewed and broaden that connection between heaven and earth so that Your will is done on earth (and in my life) as it is in heaven. Thank you Father.

Nehemiah said, *"Go and enjoy choice food and sweet drinks, and send some to those who have nothing prepared. This day is holy to our Lord. Do not grieve, for the joy of the Lord is your strength." (Nehemiah 8:10)*

Amen

No Regrets

Sweeping the kitchen floor requires only a couple brain cells, so the others can ruminate at will. After reverberating like a guitar string for several days with the implications of the Lord's joy and what that could mean to me, a stray thought flew through my head. I began to wonder what all the hurtful, difficult events of my life looked like from God's viewpoint. Not more than a couple hours later, I gasped, because I was suddenly looking at it!

When God reveals His perspective to me it is a global experience. By that I mean He uses all my senses, and seems to download revelation directly into them. It can take only a moment in actual time but might require days —or even weeks—for my mind to unravel and fit into a linear frame of reference that I can fully understand. Finding adequate vocabulary to describe it is also monumental task.

During one of those "download times," I realized my own perceptions were being re-focused. (Romans 12:2) It was like looking through one of those viewfinders you find at scenic sites along the roadside. While I was aware of the kitchen in my peripheral vision, I could see through this "heavenly telescope," a clear landscape of my past. There, in my central vision, I could even see the various directions I had taken. The goals I had, as well as the hurtful events that prevented me from attaining those goals.

I could also see that—although I would grieve over the losses—after some time, I would recover my balance, look around to see where God was moving, and continue to follow Him. From time to time (as I watched), a pang of grief—or regret over what could have been—would sting my heart. Then I would tell my Lord about it, sit with it for a while, and finally offer it to Jesus to do with as He saw fit. After a while, it seemed to me that with each nearly-attained goal so roughly taken from me, my world shrank, and my options become fewer. Still, my stance was that God is good—He had plans for me for a future and a hope. *"For I know the plans I have for you declares the Lord, plans to prosper you and not to harm you, plans to give you hope and a future" (Jeremiah 29:11).*

Thus, after a time of grieving over the '95 MS attack, I again began to assess the scope of my landscape, and tried to find what Father God would have me do. At the moment, it looked more like a playground rather than the whole wide world I had worked and traveled in before all this happened. Still, that area had seemed like nothing short of a tangle of woods when I first landed in it—a wilderness—that I was literally lost in. One I could neither see ahead, or behind me, and had no sense of direction in.

Yet, that day in the kitchen I saw each hurtful event as God saw it. That is, I saw what my life might have been like if I had stayed where I was. To my amazement, I realized I didn't really like what I saw. I kept repeating, "Thank You God! Oh, thank You, for not allowing me to stay in that place. I did not see the bigger picture—I didn't have all the pieces to the puzzle. But You could see it all. Thank You, God." I had heard it said (and had said it myself) that some day, when I could see what God saw in those events—the ones in which I could not understand why God did what He did, or allowed what transpired to happen—when I could see with His eyes, I would agree that He did the right thing. I would see, understand, and agree. It is true. I saw. I understood; and I agreed.

It was as if I were a train upon a track. I thought I had the directions for my final destination. I had a full head of steam going and was fast approaching my supposed destination. Suddenly I would be derailed by something —maybe the betrayal of a person I trusted, or by my body failing me. Each time I would regroup and put my train back on the rails, but pointed in a different direction, and do my best to work up steam again. From God's perspective, those were not derailments but course corrections. He was intent upon keeping me on the right track so that I would be able to experience the fulfillment that comes from living out my destiny. If I had continued upon my own course, I would have missed my destiny— but at the time I did not know that.

It never occurred to me that my loving Father was about the business of training me. I needed certain skill sets, knowledge, and wisdom to be able to carry out my calling. The various places I wanted to plant myself, send down my roots and live forever, were only temporary dwelling places. I was there to learn a skill and gain knowledge, not to take up a permanent residence. In His loving concern, He saw my desire to put down roots, but saw the danger in it. I was unable to hear Him gently saying, "Not here. Not yet!" Had I stayed, after I had learned the skill set or made the step in character development, I would not have been happy. I would not have been fulfilled.

But, those course corrections were nasty bumps. Normally trains slow down when they switch tracks, but I didn't know a switch was coming! I had not slowed down, so the switching of tracks felt more like a derailment than a course correction. However, looking at those events through God's eyes, I could only thank Him. Grief and regret evaporated. They were—and are—entirely gone.

Gratitude welled up within me when I saw how carefully He planned; how thoroughly He equipped me to do what He has called me to do—to make the mysteries of God plain and understandable for others. Ephesians 3:8-9 says, *"Although I am less than the least of all God's people, this grace was given me: to preach to the Gentiles the unsearchable riches of Christ, and to make plain to everyone the administration of this mystery, which for ages past was kept hidden in God, who created all things."*

Some things are becoming clearer. I thought I would be able to say that I now have a new "post-MS" vision but that is not really what it is. I have a new faith assignment. From the vantage point of God's perspective, each of the places I tried to grow roots and make my home were simply faith assignments—places to gain a skill set and hone it, places to gain wisdom and knowledge that I would need to use in the next assignment. Each assignment built upon the ones before, training and properly preparing me for my new position—which for now, is to be one step behind Jesus.

There are three reasons why He wants me one step behind Him. First, I will be close enough to hear what He says. I need to hear so I can write it down. Secondly, He does not want me to become lost. As I looked behind, I saw the way back close as I watched. The path disappeared and grass and forest grew in. It is impossible to go back; there is no path, no way. I peeked out around Jesus and looked ahead. There was no path there either! However, Jesus seemed to know where He was going and as He took one purposeful step after another, a path opened before Him. Thirdly, in His presence is the fullness of joy. In His presence I have everything I need. Living close to Him is my ultimate destiny—why not start living that destiny now! Why wait for eternity when eternity can begin here and now?

I like this idea of faith assignments. Life is one assignment after another; there is flexibility in that; whereas there is rigidity in permanence. Assignments can be changed. When change comes in the future, I think I will be more alert, and it won't catch me by surprise or appear to be a derailment. I think I will be able to celebrate the part I played rather than grieve over what I was not allowed to finish. Looking at life (especially the difficult and confusing places) from God's perspective, removes the regret.

Ask the Holy Spirit

- Ask for His perspective on the hard places and difficult people in your life.
- Ask Him to reveal the skill set or the knowledge and experience base that you are to concentrate upon in your present assignment. (Be aware that God delights in getting two for the price of one; He may have you assigned to learn a skill set from people who are irritating or obnoxious because He is simultaneously working on some aspect of your character development—building you up to be more like Jesus! We grow stronger when there is something to push against!
- Ask for His wisdom and strategies in dealing with difficult people and situations (what to say or do, when to say or do it, and how to say or do it.) Record the thoughts and possible strategies that come to you.
- Ask Him for greater capacity, capacity for love, wisdom, patience, and endurance.

Prayer

Thank you for leading and knowing the way You planned I should go. I thank You that at the right time You reveal Your perspective on the hard places and difficult people in my life and I will see, understand and approve of what You did. I thank you in advance for Your revelation. I thank You for giving me grace each day to learn the lessons You designed and the wisdom and strategies to deal with people and situations. You do all things well and I want to be like You by having excellence in all things. Father I ask for greater capacity to love and endure, as well as capacity for more wisdom and patience.

" . . . being confident of this, that he who began a good work in you will carry it on to completion until the day of Christ. (Philippines 1:6)

Amen

My Mystery Shelf

Still, there are some things I have to put on my "mystery shelf" where I put the things I cannot explain. For instance, what about the big issue, the one in my face. Actual physical healing that can be documented and sustained. It can happen. I want to be very clear on my stance in regard to healing. I believe in it. I believe in miracles that are measurable and sustainable—that can be documented medically. I also believe that I already have my physical healing, whether it can be seen physically, or not. Because, *"...with His stripes we are healed." (Isa. Isa. 53:5b)*. Jesus already paid for my healing.

God says that if we ask "according to His will" we can know that He hears us (1 John 5:14). Throughout the gospels you can read account after account of Jesus healing people. Mark 1:40-41 tells of "A man with leprosy [a] came to him and begged him on his knees, "If you are willing, you can make me clean." Jesus was moved with compassion. [b] He reached out his hand and touched the man. "I am willing," he said. "Be clean!"

Matthew 7:9 says, "Or what man is there of you, whom if his son asks bread, will he give him a stone?" If I ask my heavenly Father for healing, (and Scripture is clear that God's nature is to heal), would He not give it? My answer is, "Yes, He will." In Matthew 10:8 Jesus sent the disciples out to "heal the sick." Jesus would not send his disciples to do something that was not God's will.

However, I also know that I do not see the whole picture, while He does. The bottom line for me is that God is good and does not withhold any good thing. *"For the LORD God is a sun and shield; the LORD bestows favor and honor; no good thing does he withhold from those whose walk is blameless" (Psalm 84:11).* "Whose walk is blameless" ...if we know we have sin in our lives, it is easy enough to confess it and receive forgiveness and take that away from the equation. Let's say we have done that but still the healing does not come...what then?

Possibilities: It is possible that a person is not ready for it emotionally, or spiritually. We all know what happens when we walk too soon and put weight on a broken leg, or when someone is put in a position they are not equipped for. There are times when we are simply not ready to receive what we ask for; we could mishandle the gift.

A person may have a character flaw that could result in the mishandling of the gift. Take for example, the story of King Hezekiah in II Kings 1-20. Hezekiah followed the Lord and brought spiritual revival to Israel. He did some good work. When he became ill he asked the Lord to heal him, and He did. But during the years the Lord gave him, he sinned grievously by showing off the accrued wealth of the nation to the king of Babylon. He had to brag. The Lord rebuked him through the prophet Isaiah. God declared that He would bring judgment after Hezekiah's death through the king of Babylon who would carry away all that wealth. Hezekiah's response was telling. *"For he thought, 'Will there not be peace and security in my lifetime?" (II Kings 20:19)*

He was thinking that it was not his problem, so who cares! There is no record that he gave any thought about his children or grandchildren. How callous! We can ask for things we are not ready to receive or that we would mishandle. When the Lord does not answer, in some cases, He is having mercy upon us by preventing a bigger problem in the future. He knows when we are not strong enough to rightly use the gift we are asking Him to give. So, He restrains from giving out of love.

Another possibility is that something else might be going on. Daniel is another example. God immediately dispatched an angel with the answers for Daniel, but the angel was prevented from reaching him for twenty-one days due to warfare in heavenly realms. Something unseen prevented Daniel's answer. It is possible that something unseen is preventing my healing from becoming visible. I must use the resources provided me (prayer, fasting, meditation) to open the gates of heaven. I have to do the hard work of pulling the healing up or out or down or from the Kingdom of God into this world. But I believe healing is available for me; it has my name on it. I will work as hard as I am able spiritually and physically, and do what I can to cause my healing to be visible. On the way to doing that, I believe that I will pull out of the "slough of despond," that I slip into on occasion. I have faith to believe that the lack of motivation that has dogged me will dissipate, and I will walk freely in what God designed me to do. I'm talking about physically walking. Just because things look and feel impossible, or that they are not going to happen, does not mean they are!

Another possibility is that the Lord at some point may say to me, as He said to St. Paul, "My grace is sufficient." It is all that is needed to activate the power of Kingdom resources, otherwise none of us would ever get anywhere or anything—without Jesus we fall short of holy. We don't know whether Paul was ever healed of his physical affliction. Jacob was another who walked with a limp because the angel of the Lord dislocated his hip. Ouch! So it is possible that the Lord could ask me to wear MS, for His own reasons. But if He did, He would also commit to make sure that His grace would be sufficient for me to bear that affliction in such a way as to bring honor and glory to God.

At one time, the Lord spoke without words and communicated to me that He trusted me—with this disease, not to die, or give up under it, but instead to let Him bless me and others out of it. He had confidence in me being able not to loose sight of His character in the midst of the difficulties this new life imposes. So it is possible that I may reach more people with His words of life from my wheelchair than from a position of health—and because I present from a wheelchair, they can believe.

The bottom line for me is that I believe in physical healing for myself, and for others. I do not understand why it has not come to me—yet—but I acknowledge that I have a limited perspective and from that limited perspective I bow to His wisdom. I don't know all God's reasons or reasoning, but I trust Him. I know that He designed me "fearfully and wonderfully." He delights in me, and in His wisdom He trusted me to carry this disease for a time for His greater purposes for me. I am confident that He will share with me His reasons when the time is right and I will understand and approve of His process and ways. However, I am also hoping He will allow me to do whatever it takes to make His physical healing visible in my lifetime! *"I remain confident of this that I will see the goodness of the Lord in the land of the living." (Psalm 27:6)*

What about pain of illness and injury?

Attitude and focus are incredibly important. I think of my daughter's friend with rheumatoid arthritis (RA). She has chosen to be positive rather than to follow negative modeling, and she looks for the gifts she can find in spite of RA. I like that. Pain saps your energy, so you have less patience and grace... for anything or everything! She is using the affliction the same way I use mine: to propel her forward rather than to allow it to rob her of life and make her bitter. We look for what we can celebrate each day, and find joy where we can rather than focus on what is no more! RA and MS may shrink our world—our playing field—but we still have one! No one can say to us, "you don't know what it's like to suffer," because we do know, and we've chosen to look for the joy each day—and find it—despite our suffering.

I think of my old boss, who also had RA. His hands and feet were twisted almost beyond belief. He could only type by hunting and pecking—one key at a time. When he wanted to write he stuck a pen between his thumb and his fingers and pushed it around with his fist.

He walked with a decided limp, ate pain medications like they were candy, and washed them down with coffee that can only be described as a hot, corrosive liquid! He didn't know the Lord; he became gruffer and more crusty, and difficult to work with as the pain twisted his spirit as well as his hands.

I think of another friend's elderly father who had congestive heart failure. The process of dying was excruciating and slow, but every time people visited him, they came away inspired. The man kept thanking God for each and every moment of his life and blessing each and every person in his life. When doctors could no longer medicate the pain away, he simply kept saying "Jesus. Jesus. Sweet Jesus!"

I think of Zach who lost his legs when he stepped on a bomb in Afghanistan. I've lost count of his surgeries. He is a new daddy.

Pain is horrible! In the painful experience it can be so severe that it shuts down your ability to see or to hear. That's why so often we think God was not there when it happened. Or, we think that He didn't do anything to stop it.

But God is good, that is not changed by our circumstances. His character is what we need to focus on. We need to draw Him into our experience, rather than focusing on what hurts, and blaming God for causing it. He did not plant the IED that Zach stepped on. Jesus does know suffering; the crucifixion was no walk in the park. God walks through our pain with us, and transforms our pain into blessing and glory. We don't have to go through our pain alone—but He won't intrude—we have to ask Him to be with us.

Heaven's way of doing things is different from our ways and we have a hard time wrapping our minds around it. It is possible for us to learn to think God's thoughts, but like any new skill it takes practice and failing, getting up, and trying again. Many times. I want to reiterate. Pain is horrible. It hurts. That's true.

God is good ... that is also true.

Horrible things should never happen—not to anyone. But, they do. I believe that these things are directly influenced by demons—evil workers of wickedness. This was what I was trying to comprehend, to wrap my mind around, when the Lord told me it would only give me a headache, and I would contaminate my spirit by focusing on all the horrible things that were happening in the world, rather than He who is the solution.

As for the individuals who have been victimized by any of these evils, my first response is to validate your experience. Yes, it was—and still is—horrible. It should never have happened. You have every right to be angry. I would be too. And so is God. The question is: "What are you going to do with that anger?

What happened to us shattered our lives—we will never be the same—we have been altered. We have to live with the damage done to us. However, that does not mean we cannot have a life and a destiny. It will simply be different than what could have been. Different than God's original design. The fact that you are reading these words is proof of survival. It means God still has a purpose and a plan for you—for good—for a hope and a future (Jeremiah 9:11). I am glad we survived and are still here. Our job is to find the pieces of our lives, clean them up, figure out God's plan, then work with Him to put things back together. Let's get going again! He is God, and He can make "all things new" (Corinthians 5:17).

I choose to say, "Lord, I give this thing that has happened to me, to You. I trust Your judgment." Note, here, to those who find themselves in their wilderness place due to someone else's horrible actions or abuse of them. They can ask Him to accomplish forgiveness in them, because on our own own we can't forgive such evil. Recognize that we must forgive; otherwise we are still connected to the thing, and the bitterness will eat us alive. Forgiveness disconnects us. Then we can put it on our "mystery shelf." That's where I put all the things I cannot explain. It's how I maintain sanity in an increasingly insane world!

I believe the bottom line is that we all need to do some difficult work, ourselves. For me it is to continue with exercise and keeping mobile. St. Paul references athletes and the training they subject themselves to. He talks about "running our race and buffeting our bodies" (doing difficult things—for a prize), and showing ourselves to be worthy workmen. What is difficult will be specific to the challenge we each face. We all find ourselves in different circumstances and walking through different kinds of wilderness. We may all feel that our situation and our challenges are unique. But again, St. Paul would say, "Nah, no temptation, no challenge you face is so unique that it's never been faced. Rather it is "common" to man."

In his words: *"No temptation has overtaken you except what is common to mankind. And God is faithful; he will not let you be tempted beyond what you can bear. But when you are tempted, he will also provide a way out so that you can endure it. (I Corinthians 10:13)* With the temptation (to give in, to quit, roll up in a fetal position) there is a way out. He does not promise that it will be easy. However, we are built to do hard things. We can do this.

My experience is that we can begin to find out what our tasks are by asking The Holy Spirit questions and then using the grace God gives us, daily, to act on His responses. Acting on what The Holy Spirit communicates to us will deepen our intimacy with God, and make our lives different.

Ask the Holy Spirit

- Where were You, God when this event happened? What were You doing?
- Where are You, God, in this circumstance now?
- Please show me where I have been withholding forgiveness. From whom?
- What do I do with my anger? Do I lash out at others, or turn it inward against myself (depression)?
- Against whom have I been harboring a slow simmering resentment?
- Am I complaining against You, God, when I complain against my circumstances? (1 Corinthians 10:1-11)
- Holy Spirit please show me changes I need to make in attitude and focus.
- Am I holding on to dysfunction or immaturity? Or am I enabling someone else's dysfunction or immaturity?

➤ What habits would You help me build in that would enable my own and others functionality and maturity?

Prayer

Thank you God for being present when (this happened) to me even though I could not see you nor feel Your presence. I confess that there is a lot I do not understand but I invite you into my circumstances now. Please be present with me in my current situation. Help me feel your presence with me. I pray you give me wisdom for what to say and what to choose. Help me to see my circumstances with Your eyes. Show me where I am withholding forgiveness and then give me the strength to forgive. I have not had much modeling on how to do it, or what to do with my anger. Forgive me for lashing out and then for beating up on myself, and slipping into depression. I know that neither one of those things is honoring to You.

Teach me how to be angry and yet not to sin. Reveal to me any habitual ways of dealing with anger so that I do not hurt others, or myself. Teach me self-control so that the words I speak honor You; help me not to complain. Holy Spirit, please show me changes I need to make in attitude and focus so that I am not holding on to dysfunction, or immaturity. Help me build the spiritual habits and body memory reflexes that would enable intimacy with you, functionality, and maturity. God, You are good.

"Therefore, since we are surrounded by such a great

cloud of witnesses, let us throw off everything that hinders and the sin that so easily entangles. And let us run with perseverance the race marked out for us."

(Hebrews 12:1)

"Praise be to the God and Father of our Lord Jesus Christ, the Father of compassion and the God of all comfort, who comforts us in all our troubles, so that we can comfort those in any trouble with the comfort we ourselves have received from God."

(2 Corinthians 1:3, 4).

"One thing I ask from the Lord, this only do I seek: that I may dwell in the house of the Lord all the days of my life, to gaze on the beauty of the Lord and to seek him in his temple."

(Psalm 27:4)

Amen

My Long Sleep

Awakening after five months of sleeping twelve to sixteen hours a day, I went into shock. The MS attack had done something to my plumbing! Fifty pounds of fluid had accumulated over my entire body. None of my clothing fit; I did not want to go shopping for new clothes. I was not going to be that big, end of discussion. I had two or three articles of clothing that I could wear—so I did, over and over again! There is a cartoon of The Pink Panther in which he steps into a shower and the water goes inside his pink suit instead of down the drain. The water sloshed and squished when he walked. He left wet footprints on the floor. That is how I felt.

With my husband's assistance I found a massage therapist trained in Manual Lymph Drainage; she greatly reduced the fluid. The cause, however, was MS and that she could not reverse. I needed to know the spiritual significance of these difficulties! I also needed to know what, in my life, was waste which I had not properly eliminated. It may have been good at one time, but had long since become of no value. It was no longer life-giving.

The Lord is such a good teacher! Before instructing me, He assured me that nothing I had done for Him was waste. Nothing that I had entrusted to Him was waste. Then He put words to some things I sensed but for which I had no words. It helped me understand the emotional turmoil I was experiencing.

The Lord showed me that He gave the ability to build defense mechanisms but there was one in particular that was helpful in the past that I needed to take out of the category of automatic, knee jerk responses. It was only to be used with great discretion—only at the Lord's direction. That response was to withdraw and shut down and cut off a relationship. This automatic shut down response was something that was to be eliminated! It was not only causing physical problems, but spiritual as well. It served a purpose in the past, but was no longer to be the response of first recourse. He invited me to spend time with Him to retool that reflex.

A second thing I needed to eliminate was our house. The Lord had blessed us with a wonderful home in which to raise our daughters. It was given to us for a season and the time of that blessing was over. He called us into new things, new blessings. I had said that I would need a direct word from the Lord that was as clear as was the giving of the house before I would be willing to release it. This particular conversation with the Lord was that direct word. He helped me understand that to refuse to release the home He gave us when He called us to something else, would be to love the gift more than the giver. It would be like withholding the fatty portion of the offering that had been dedicated to the Lord. I grieved, and in obedience we sold our house! If I had been unwilling to learn new reflexes, or if I had hung onto the house, it would have, in some way, poisoned my relationship with my Lord!

Additionally, I needed to track down any attitudes, feelings, or behaviors that would poison my own spirit and relationship with others. I needed to discover what to take in and what to avoid in order to maintain spiritual health and cleanliness. The problem with elimination difficulties is that a person can poison their own body if waste is not eliminated in a timely fashion.

When your body breaks out whether it be with a rash, acne, boils, psoriasis or eczema, that is your body letting you know that something is not right. You have taken in something you should not, something that does not agree with you. The Lord showed me that I can break out with a spiritual rash around arrogance, small-mindedness, religiosity, two-facedness, and self-centeredness. Seeing and hearing of misogyny hurts me. If I am devalued and deemed less, simply because I'm a woman, or if others treat my input as if it's of inferior quality, that is painful. It hurts me to see someone else suffer from misogyny as well. When spiritual toxins are not eliminated or cleansed, they affect the physical body which begins to break down. It seemed clear to me that I needed to make sure I did not have to endure an environment of misogyny for very long.

When I awoke from my long sleep, another feature I had to contend with was numbness. Either I could not feel or I experienced inaccurate feelings. My feet often feel like they are freezing cold but if I touch them with my hands they might be cool but by no means cold. So I asked the Lord about it and the response I sensed was that spiritual numbness does not just give you inaccurate messages, it ensures that you do not receive any message at all. No messages of love or encouragement to sustain or equip you, no messages for the healing, building up, or encouragement of The Body either. Numbness is very dangerous and debilitating.

Sensitivity can be restored by pouring out our hearts to Him—to just spend time with Him hanging out. We don't need to pray for anything, or intercede. We only need to sit with Him. When thoughts come to us, we should share them with Him. If we have no thoughts, we can share that.

A second thing I can do is to find a faithful friend, who is on the same journey, and share what the Lord and I talk about. Share my troubles and confusions, my cutting edge, and my glory stories—the neat things God does for me in the day to day, when I look for Him.

Sharing troubles helps us not to feel so alone in our journey of becoming sons and daughters. When we share our cutting edge—we just may be able to help each other. Sharing our glory stories we encourage, build each other up, and delight our Father's heart.

In my walk with the Lord one precaution I can take not to lose sensitivity again is to stay close to Him and always share my heart with Him. In talking-with-God time, I learned that if I write out what I hear from the Lord I will have a harder time discounting and dismissing His words to me. It will be more difficult to convince myself that I was listening to my imagination. Doubt, He showed me, was the issue. Along with doubt comes discouragement, which clouds vision and drains off spiritual strength.

Doubt makes us vulnerable to insecurities and fears and we become snared by the "cares of this world." We begin to fret and worry. When I worry it uses up my energies and throws a wet blanket on my enjoyment of life which leads to losing my sense of humor and perspective. Without energy, joy, or humor I have little left over to invest in my particular assignment within Jesus's larger work of reconciliation. And my God loves getting a great ROI—return on investment—in me!

Sometimes outside circumstances require huge energy output. Other times the fretting and worry use it up, and sometimes I have simply used my little bit in living. Any time these three elements are combined in some way, the drain is faster. These are the times tiredness becomes painful, and it takes days for the energies to return—and even more time before the joy returns. Like a slow spring that I must monitor so it is not overused and drained dry, I must monitor energies to keep a consistent supply. Bluntly put—if you over-use, you self-abuse. The Lord was very clear—fretting needed to stop. He and I needed to work on the fears and insecurities, and the sources of doubt. These were weak places in my trust.

Another big thing I learned in meditation, was that seeing myself as insignificant also affected my hearing. It muffled God's voice. In some part of me was a belief that someone as magnificent as God would not be interested in speaking to one as insignificant as I. My belief in my insignificance also influenced the conclusions I came to when I did hear His voice. His voice became to me like background noise—I paid it little attention. I learned that I entertained a fear that I might actually hear Him ... and then what? That "Selah" moment brought deep repentance! For me, it took the time of meditation and asking God specific questions and writing down the thoughts that came into my mind, to reveal these things to me.

Now, as a matter of obedience, I am to share with David (my husband), and prayer partners the Lord assigns, what I hear in my time with the Lord. Accountability strengthens my confidence in self as well as in the Lord. I felt the Lord encourage David and me to be more disciplined about doing what we knew in regard to spiritual hygiene. By that I mean to pray for cleansing when we have been out and about in the world, or in spiritual realms praying or counseling with someone, lest something unholy follow us home!

Normally when we think of discipline we think it cannot be much fun. The Lord challenged me to be more disciplined in feeding my spirit, lest I exhaust the strength of my soul. I was happy to do that. Feeding my spirit is fun! I do that with art and music. So God wanted me to return to painting or playing the piano or getting dirty with clay.

I confess, I haven't done much painting, and playing the piano is difficult because of all the eye movement. Other muscles also quickly fatigue; after a few minutes my back muscles scream at me. However, ten minutes of music is ten more than I would have had if I hadn't stopped and played!

 ## Ask the Holy Spirit

> ➢ Ask the Lord if you need to supplement your

spiritual diet.
- How does God want you to change your spiritual diet. It's not only about what you need to cut out, but also about what you need to add in.
- What interferes with communication between God and me?
- Why do I not hear Your directions or, in hearing them, why do I interpret them incorrectly?
- What sin hides within me waiting for a weak moment to strike?
- What responses to sin in my life "chew me up" and "eat me alive?"
- How do these responses interfere with my relationship with You, God, and the work You have designed for me to do?
- What causes my energies to come and go, to be drained away, so that life becomes a burden and all joy is gone?
- What activities and/or responses need to be changed or modified?
- What changes can I make to maximize the energies I have so that I honor and glorify You and bless those I live with and relate to?
- What am I spiritually sensitive to or allergic to?
- What do I need to cut down on or eliminate from my life?
- What is the "fat" I am holding onto—either the sin or the "fatty portion," the thing of great value, that is Yours, but I am keeping for myself?
- Where am I spiritually numb either from my own pain or from being filled up with the pain of others?

- What are the inaccurate messages I receive as a result of the numbness? How can feeling be restored?
- In my walk with You what precautions can I put in place so that I do not lose sensitivity again?

Prayer

Father you have called me by name and I have followed. Thank you for pursuing me and not giving up on me. Thank you for walking with me in my wilderness and showing me your paths, for teaching me your ways; for preparing a future and a destiny for me. Thank you for showing me what needs to go so that I can more closely align with your purposes. You amaze me.

"Show me your ways, Lord, teach me your paths. Guide me in your truth and teach me, for you are God my Savior, and my hope is in you all day long." (Psalm 25:4-5)

Amen

Camel Hair Shirt

I don't know about you, but camelhair shirts really give me a rash! Maybe I'm allergic to camelhair. I hadn't even realized I was wearing one until one day my writing partner suggested several radical measures to take on the piece I was writing. She was absolutely right, but after the phone call I carried on like the camel from which my shirt was made! I bellowed my objections that the load was too heavy. The way was far too long. I moaned and groaned. I whined and carried on!

Just as my lament was reaching its crescendo, the Lord stood before me. He didn't raise His voice. There was no sarcasm in His tone. He just stood there as Commander in Chief, as Lord. And He said, "You said you wanted to learn everything I have to teach you."

The truth of His words took my breath away. I fell to my knees. I was undone by my own words. He was right. Absolutely right!

When I first awakened after the initial long sleep of MS (five months), many people wanted to pray for my healing. I let them. When I was not healed right away, another round of caring folk suggested first one healer and then another. I went to hear some of them, but always had to leave before much of anything happened. I don't know why healing can't occur in the church before 9:00 or 10:00 p.m.

There was always hesitancy in me. A kind of knowing that the Lord was going to use the MS somehow for His glory and my benefit. That doesn't make sense, I know, but God's logic is quite different from human logic, and His values turn our values on end. I don't understand either. But I told someone that I wanted to milk this experience with the disease for all it was worth. They were shocked, so I explained that I was not in a hurry to receive my healing because I wanted to learn everything God had to teach me during this time. I did not want to do another lap around the Sinai.

This stance was probably the source of the hesitancy in me about healing prayer. I wanted to learn whatever I could on the first try, and I didn't want to receive healing prematurely lest I miss a lesson that I or someone else would need! I never doubted God's ability to heal me. What I doubted was my own ability to know His timing, to recognize the optimum time to ask Him for what He had died to give me!

As the Lord repeated my own words back to me, they hit with such a force I stopped mid-whine. Something happened inside me. The whine was gone. All I could say was, "Yes, Lord." At that moment I felt complaining was over and done—I could rub liniment on when arduous work made me sore, but not complain! Never again!

That was when I realized that underneath the robe of

righteousness the Lord had given me was a camelhair shirt. I asked Him, "Why the shirt? I can't get it off."

He explained that He provided the resources I would need when I accepted His calling.

I was incredulous! "I need this hot, smelly, irritating undershirt?"

He didn't respond to the question, just kept talking. "Every calling has its task(s). You are to engage the tasks, but as you do, the tasks will work on you, building, and shaping you into the fullness of the character of Christ. The work and the disciplines of your calling is your camelhair shirt. The things in and about that calling which poke and irritate the flesh, these are my gifts to you."

I stood there with my mouth hanging open. If I understand Him correctly, writing and the rigors of MS are my "shirt." If I am to learn all the Lord has to teach me, I will submit to those disciplines. I guess once a camel, always a camel. Sad to say, once the initial shock wore off, I again skated right back into complaining. Like Rudyard Kipling's camel, I "humphed."

I found I moved into the flesh in ways I had been unaware of. The work of writing pokes and jabs, as do the people with whom I live and work. My flesh is irritatingly brought to light—sometimes raw from the chaffing, like an untended saddle sore. I am thinking, probably all flesh is allergic to camelhair and spiritual disciplines!

I have some choices to make at this point. I can choose to repent, forgive, and heal. I can choose to put flesh to death in relationship to others and the Lord. I can choose to grow in capacity to love like Jesus. I can choose to submit to the disciplines of my calling. Or I can moan and groan and carry on like a camel. I am finding that as

I do the nasty work of putting flesh to death, the camel hairs irritate less. The disciplines—the parameters of my calling, even the people with whom I work—become the banks through which my spirit flows. They are part of defining my limits and boundaries, but they are not barriers that restrict or hem me in. Rather, they give direction and purpose to my life. They become the avenues through which others are blessed—to God's glory and my benefit.

When I begin to overheat, it usually is not the camelhair shirt or any spiritual discipline causing the problem. I tend to overheat when I move too quickly. I can't seem to sprint, like an Olympic athlete, down the lane set before me—too much friction from my shirt. My flesh is poked, reminding me not to move that way. Because of the disciplines, I come to know The Holy Spirit who encourages me to proceed at His pace, to stand straighter and walk taller, more like Jesus. That irritating gift keeps me on task. It helps me remember what I am doing and why.

When I tire and collapse in a heap—when my shoulders melt down into my hips—my body doesn't fit the shirt properly, and the goofy thing starts poking. When I lean into the flesh the camel hairs encourage me to straighten up, to move and walk in the ways of the Lord. But until I learn to submit to Father-filtered problems and learn how to find resources within (or without) to solve those problems, this darned camelhair shirt is going to keep on giving me a rash!

Every problem in your life is Father-filtered. Nothing escapes your Father's watchful eye. Therefore, if a problem exists in your life, not only is it there for you to solve, but it is in some way for your good. Learning how to solve the problem will build something into you that you did not know you needed. If you turn to Him with the irritation, Jesus will help you find the resources that are hidden within you and give you the strategy to turn them into pearls, just like an oyster coats an irritating grain of sand turning it into a pearl! The irritated place is the very place where He wants to create something of beauty and value.

Ask the Holy Spirit

- What is the irritant in your life that God may be calling you to turn into a pearl?
- That stressful situation is one of the resources God has given you to help you to grow and develop into the person He designed you to be. Ask God to show you the humorous and to keep you in good humor.
- Ask Him for His strategy for growing in the stressful moment and changing the sand into a pearl.
- Ask Him to help you see the resources you need to do it!

Prayer

Lord, in this moment of clarity I thank you for the irritating people and the disciplines that poke, stretch and challenge me. And I thank you for the process of grinding away what has covered over the treasures you have hidden in me and those against whom I rub and chafe as you polish us. I know that one day I will be able to thank you from a place of seeing what you have done, but during the process I thank you by faith.

Mold me, melt me, fill me, and use me. I dare to praise you in the presence of my enemies. Your plans for me are wondrous. Thank you Father.

"I will give you hidden treasures, riches stored in secret places, so that you may know that I am the Lord, the God of Israel, who summons you by name." (Isaiah 45:3)

"My goal is...that they may know Christ, in whom are hidden all the treasures of wisdom and knowledge."
(Colossians 2:2-3)

Amen

Dear Reader...

This book has become a call to the Body of Christ to look again at the hard places in life with a different framework, a different perspective, a different set of lenses. Why are those hard things, the betrayals, the seeming failures, the pain and losses and the inexplicable craziness that came out of nowhere, permitted by the hand of a loving father! Is he allowing or is He, in incredibly miraculous ways, getting us out of situations we brought on ourselves?

Maybe He has had a better plan for us all along, and can use even these things to bring His dreams for us to pass. If only we would turn ourselves wholly over to Him for some "heavenly rehabilitation."

Even as we prune fruit trees to produce more fruit—there are times when we, too, must endure some necessary "cutting away" of those things which have hindered our growth. In the same way, athletes lift heavier and heavier weights, and repetitively do the same exercise to develop muscle memory or to make muscles grow. We push promising athletes so they develop reflexes, and we also pile responsibilities on the son who shows promise. Is it inconceivable, then, that a holy God would use whatever adversity opposes us, for good instead of evil, and to instead develop in us the spiritual muscles which are needed not only to overcome evil, but to love his presence and his will in our lives even more?

In my own journey "through the wilderness" with MS, I have discovered that even though God lovingly walks with us every step of the way, we must still make the choice to exercise the faith that makes us want to spend time with God and praise him, regardless of our outward circumstance.

I am right there with Paul when he says, *"Not that I have already obtained all this, or have already been made perfect, but I press on to take hold of that for which Christ Jesus took hold of me." (Phil 3:12)* We are always a work in progress until we stand before our King!

If you have made the decision that holiness and relationship with Jesus are more important than how you feel at any given moment, just keep slogging toward Him —make Him your goal! Then go through one hard thing after another without letting go of that goal, knowing that enduring will build His very own nature and character into you, until you are like Him. Always remembering that *"His divine power has given us everything we need for a godly life through our knowledge of Him who called us by His own glory and goodness," (2 Peter 1:3)*

Of course, understanding the concepts is easier than building new skills, attitudes, and habits. The process of building skills and reflexes takes time and practice. The

Lord knows that and gives us an entire lifetime to practice. I'm not there yet, but God has assured me that the end result will be holiness—and as a bonus—razor sharp discernment. Hebrews 5:14 describes those who build in the skills and habits of holiness as those *"who by reason of use have their senses exercised to discern both good and evil."* By reason of use is another way of saying "practice."

As the days grow darker and our Lord's return comes ever closer, we will need that razor sharp discernment to tell the difference between good and evil. God lovingly prepares the environment (the spiritual gym) for us to practice in, but we must choose to actually go there. To exercise our bodies, senses, and our spirits to develop the skills and reflexes of holiness that will be so valuable to us in the days ahead.

Even so, change can be a challenge, and our fear of it (or denial of the need to change in ways that lead to holiness) will only make it harder. My hope is that sharing my experiences will encourage you to look at your own life differently. That you will rise up and put your shoulder to the experiences God allows in your life and lean into those hard things like a dedicated athlete!

Remember how the Lord can use all the hard experiences of life to carve away what hinders His holiness from being visible in the lives of His saints. He is the one that changes and transforms us—like sand against stones in a rock tumbler wear away what obscures the gem within. He can turn dimly glowing lamps into crystal chandeliers that refract the light of His Glory. Or rainbows of light and color that can fill the room!

When first diagnosed with MS, I did not understand,

and God did not tell me, that this disease could be a part of His transformation of an earthen vessel into a vessel that could not only hold His glory but radiate it for the whole world to see. I did not understand, and He did not tell me, that although the adversary meant my harm, He (God) would use my struggle to hold onto the faith in Him that would make room in my life for His holiness, His Glory! He can use the hard stuff of life to carve away all that does not look like Jesus, all that obscures His light from shining. He transforms us; He sanctifies us and it is Him who makes us holy!

How this process of sanctification that leads to holiness looks in your life will be different than mine, but the results will be the same. Don't give up! I promise there will come a time as you journey through your wilderness (whatever that might be) when you will see the glory, and hear His voice for yourself. Even as Moses did so long ago when he first encountered God in his wilderness, and was called to actually step into His presence. *"...When the Lord saw that he had gone over to look, God called to him from within the bush, "Moses! Moses!"*

And Moses said, "Here I am."

"Do not come any closer," God said. "Take off your sandals, for the place where you are standing is holy ground." (Exodus 3: 4-5)

Since then, God has continued to call out to His people through the generations. He is calling to you and me. But whether or not we answer that call is up to us. He will never take away our right to choose. Yet, He will always encourage us to choose Him. *"Today I ask heaven and earth to be witnesses. I am offering you life or death, blessings or curses. Now, choose life! Then you and your children may live." (Deuteronomy 30:19).*

About fifteen hundred years later, the apostle Peter put it this way: *"Therefore, preparing your minds for action, and being sober-minded, set your hope fully on the grace that will be brought to you at the revelation of Jesus Christ. As obedient children, do not be conformed to the passions of your former ignorance, but as he who called you is holy, you also be holy..." (1Peter 13:15)*

Maybe you're struggling through wilderness places of your own, right now, or going through some fire of affliction. If so, your spiritual muscles are getting a workout. Never forget that God's design is to make you strong and healthy and more in love with him than ever. The wilderness takes many forms. Even a lovely home or apartment with a manicured garden can be a wilderness at times. But if you ask to see your circumstances with God's eyes, you will see beauty and find refreshment there, too. God can lead you through the wilderness... but only if you let Him!

In A Quiet Place

In a quiet place,
hidden away,
out of reach of the gardener's hand,
walking on a sunbeam, a spider spins her silken thread.
She forms a lovely net to catch the morning dew.
Silken webs hold each drop securely.
She'll return another time,
To drink her fill.

My home's a quiet place,
hidden away,
Out of the reach of needy souls.
Weaving thoughts together, the Lord and I stand on my balcony.
We form a loving net to catch the Father's jewels,
Transcribing each one neatly.
I return many times,
To drink my fill.

"Be of good courage and he shall strengthen your heart, all you that hope in the LORD."
PSALM 31:24

ABOUT THE AUTHOR

Carol A. Brown is the author of six books, including the popular, *Mystery of Spiritual Sensitivity*, which has been translated into four languages. She is also the author of the *Sassy Pants Learns* series, in which she distills some of the more mysterious truths of life into the language of children. Carol and her husband live in Michigan, and have been in Christian ministry for many years. They have two daughters, five grandchildren, and a great-grandson. You can get in touch with her through her website at:

CarolABrown.com

Other Books By

Carol A. Brown

For Adults:

The Mystery of Spiritual Sensitivity

Highly Sensitive

For Children:

Sassy Pants Learns

Sassy Pants Learns How To Make Amends

Sassy Pants Learns About Strange Creatures

www.ingramcontent.com/pod-product-compliance
Lightning Source LLC
Chambersburg PA
CBHW070052120526
44588CB00033B/1412